lonely planet

PROVENCE
& SOUTHEAST
FRANCE

ROAD
TRIPS

Oliver Berry, Jean-Bernard Carillet,
Gregor Clark, Hugh McNaughtan, Nicola Williams

HOW TO USE THIS BOOK

Reviews

In the Destinations section:

All reviews are ordered in our writers' preference, starting with their most preferred option. Additionally:

Sights are arranged in the geographic order that we suggest you visit them and, within this order, by writer preference.

Eating and Sleeping reviews are ordered by price range (budget, midrange, top end) and, within these ranges, by writer preference.

Map Legend

Routes
- Trip Route
- Trip Detour
- Linked Trip
- Walk Route
- Tollway
- Freeway
- Primary
- Secondary
- Tertiary
- Lane
- Unsealed Road
- Plaza/Mall
- Steps
-)=(Tunnel
- Pedestrian Overpass
- Walk Track/Path

Boundaries
- International
- State/Province
- Cliff

Hydrography
- River/Creek
- Intermittent River
- Swamp/Mangrove
- Canal
- Water
- Dry/Salt/ Intermittent Lake
- Glacier

Highway Markers
- [A20] Highway marker

Trips
- 1 Trip Numbers
- 9 Trip Stop
- Walking tour
- Trip Detour

Population
- ✪ Capital (National)
- ◉ Capital (State/Province)
- ● City/Large Town
- ● Town/Village

Areas
- Beach
- Glacier
- Cemetery (Christian)
- Cemetery (Other)
- Park
- Forest
- Reservation
- Urban Area
- Sportsground

Transport
- ✈ Airport
- Cable Car/ Funicular
- Ⓜ Metro station
- Ⓟ Parking
- Train/Railway
- Tram

Note: Not all symbols displayed above appear on the maps in this book

Symbols In This Book

- ✓ Top Tips
- 🍷 Food & Drink
- Link Your Trips
- 🌳 Outdoors
- Tips from Locals
- 📷 Essential Photo
- Trip Detour
- 🏃 Walking Tour
- History & Culture
- ✕ Eating
- Family
- 🛏 Sleeping

- ◉ Sights
- 🛏 Sleeping
- 🏖 Beaches
- ✕ Eating
- 🏃 Activities
- 🍷 Drinking
- 🎓 Courses
- ☆ Entertainment
- ☞ Tours
- 🛍 Shopping
- 🎉 Festivals & Events
- ℹ Information & Transport

These symbols and abbreviations give vital information for each listing:

- ✆ Telephone number
- ✆ Pet-friendly
- ☺ Opening hours
- 🚌 Bus
- P Parking
- ⛴ Ferry
- ⊝ Nonsmoking
- 🚊 Tram
- ❄ Air-conditioning
- 🚆 Train
- @ Internet access
- apt apartments
- 📶 Wi-fi access
- d double rooms
- 🏊 Swimming pool
- dm dorm beds
- 🥗 Vegetarian selection
- q quad rooms
- r rooms
- 📖 English-language menu
- s single rooms
- ste suites
- 👪 Family-friendly
- tr triple rooms
- tw twin rooms

CONTENTS

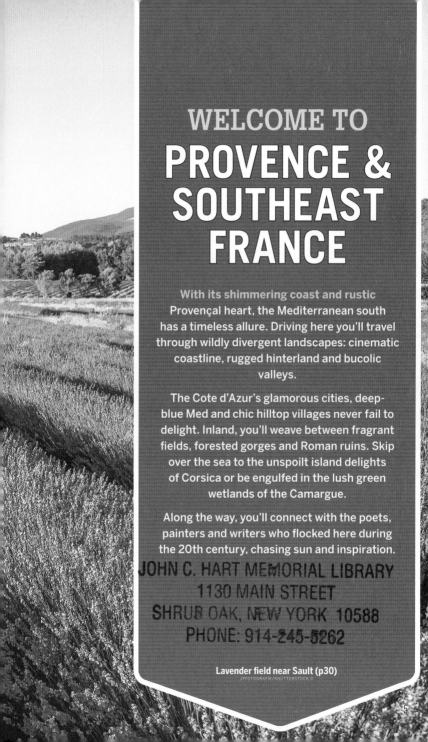

WELCOME TO
PROVENCE & SOUTHEAST FRANCE

With its shimmering coast and rustic Provençal heart, the Mediterranean south has a timeless allure. Driving here you'll travel through wildly divergent landscapes: cinematic coastline, rugged hinterland and bucolic valleys.

The Cote d'Azur's glamorous cities, deep-blue Med and chic hilltop villages never fail to delight. Inland, you'll weave between fragrant fields, forested gorges and Roman ruins. Skip over the sea to the unspoilt island delights of Corsica or be engulfed in the lush green wetlands of the Camargue.

Along the way, you'll connect with the poets, painters and writers who flocked here during the 20th century, chasing sun and inspiration.

Lavender field near Sault (p30)
JFFOTOGRAFIE/SHUTTERSTOCK ©

1 **Roman Provence**
Fabulous scenery and well-preserved Roman buildings make history come alive. **3 DAYS**

2 **Lavender Route**
Fine picnic spots and picturesque hilltop villages are filled with the scent of lavender. **4-5 DAYS**

4 **The Camargue**
Wetlands, wildlife and a sense of wonder: it's all here in the Camargue. **4 DAYS**

Die
Parc Naturel Régional du Vercors
DRÔME
Valreas
Rhône
Pont-St-Esprit
Vaison-la-Romaine
PROVENCE
Mont Ventoux (1912m)
Orange
VAUCLUSE
Carpentras
Durance
GARD
Pont du Gard
Sorgues
Avignon
Forcalquie
Gard
Coustellet
Gordes
Parc Naturel Régional du Luberon
Nîmes
Noves
St-Rémy de Provence
Mourre Nègre (1125m)
Caissargues
Tarascon
Glanum
Orgon
Cadenet
St-Gilles
Arles
Salon-de-Provence
Pelissanne
Durance
St-Chamas
Aix-en-Provence
Parc Naturel Régional de Camargue
Étang de Berre
St-Maximin-la-Ste-Baume
Stes-Maries-de-la-Mer
Port St-Louis du Rhône
L'Estaque
Marseille
Aubagne
Golfe de Beauduc
Cassis
Les Lecques
MEDITERRANEAN SEA

PROVENCE & SOUTHEAST FRANCE

★

Parc National des Ecrins

Parc Naturel Regional du Queyras

HAUTES-ALPES

Gap

Embrun

Seyne-les-Alpes

Le Sauze

St Etienne-la-Tinée

Reserve Geologique de Haute Provence

La Javie

Colmars-les-Alpes

Parc National du Mercantour

St-Sauveur-sur-Tinee

St-Martin-Vesubie

Château-Arnoux St-Auban

ALPES DE HAUTE-PROVENCE

ALPES-MARITIMES

Roquebillière

es Mées

Villars-sur-Var

ITALY

âteau de lensole

Parc Naturel Régional du Verdon

Loup

Vence

Ventimiglia

MONACO ★

Menton

Artuby

Grasse

Nice

Argens

Antibes

Cannes

Fréjus

St-Raphaël

VAR

St-Maxime

MEDITERRANEAN SEA

Cuers

St-Tropez

3 **Modern Art Meander**
See works by famous artists and the places that inspired them. **7 DAYS**

ulon Hyères

Le Lavandou

48km to Corsica

Ⓝ 0 ———————— 40 km
   0 ———————— 20 miles

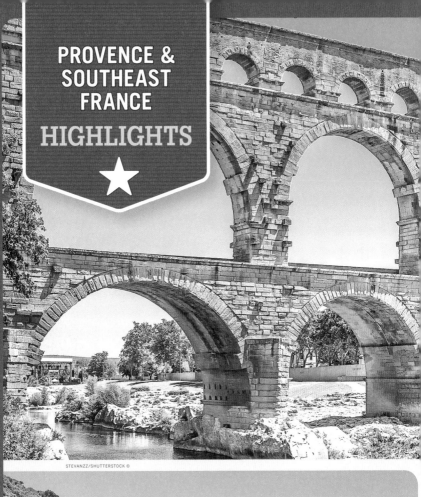

PROVENCE & SOUTHEAST FRANCE

HIGHLIGHTS

★

STEVANZZ/SHUTTERSTOCK ©

Pont du Gard (above) The scale of this Roman aqueduct is astonishing. View it from the banks of the Gard River, clamber along the top deck, or see it lit up after dark. See it on Trip **1**

The Camargue (right) This huge natural wetland is a paradise for nature lovers, with its incredible birdlife, wild horses and outrageous pink flamingos. See it on Trip **4**

Abbaye Notre-Dame de Sénanque (left) Still home to a small number of monks, this remote and beautiful 12th-century Cistercian abbey is famously framed by lavender fields. See it on Trip **2**

CITY GUIDE

PARIS

If ever a city needed no introduction, it's Paris – a trend setter, fashion former and style icon for centuries, and it is still very much at the cutting edge. Whether you're here to tick off the landmarks or seek out the secret corners, Paris fulfils all your expectations, and still leaves you wanting more.

Eiffel Tower, Paris

Getting Around

Driving in Paris is a nightmare. Happily, there's no need for a car. The metro is fast, frequent and efficient; tickets cost €1.90 (day passes from €7.50) and are valid on the city's buses. Bikes can be hired from 1800 Vélib (www.velib.paris.fr) stations; insert a credit card, authorise a €300 deposit and pedal away. Day passes cost €5; first 30 minutes free, subsequent 30 minutes from €1.

Parking

Meters don't take coins; use a chip-enabled credit card. Municipal car parks cost €2 to €6 an hour, or €20 to €36 per 24 hours.

Where to Eat

Le Marais is one of the best areas for eating out, with its small restaurants and trendy bistros. Don't miss Paris' street markets: the Marché Bastille, rue Montorgueil and rue Mouffetard are full of atmosphere.

Where to Stay

Base yourself in Montmartre for its Parisian charm, if you don't mind crowds. Le Marais and Bastille provide style on a budget, while St-Germain is good for a splurge.

Useful Websites

Paris Info (http://en.parisinfo.com) Official visitor site.

Lonely Planet (www.lonelyplanet.com/paris) Lonely Planet's city guide.

Secrets of Paris (www.secretsofparis.com) Local's blog full of insider tips.

Paris by Mouth (www.parisbymouth.com) Eat and drink your way around the capital.

For more, check out our city and country guides. www.lonelyplanet.com

TOP EXPERIENCES

➡ Eiffel Tower at Twilight
Any time is a good time to take in the panorama from the top of the 'MetalAsparagus' (as Parisians snidely call it) – but the twilight view is extra special (www.toureiffel.fr).

➡ Musée du Louvre
France's greatest repository of art, sculpture and artefacts, the Louvre is a must-visit – but don't expect to see it all in a day (www.louvre.fr).

➡ Basilique du Sacré-Coeur
Climb inside the cupola of this Montmartre landmark for one of the best cross-city vistas (www.sacre-coeur-montmartre.com).

➡ Musée d'Orsay
Paris' second-most-essential museum, with a fabulous collection encompassing originals by Cézanne, Degas, Monet, Van Gogh and more (www.musee-orsay.fr).

➡ Cathédrale de Notre-Dame
Peer over Paris from the north tower of this Gothic landmark, surrounded by gargoyles and flying buttresses (www.cathedraledeparis.com).

➡ Les Catacombes
Explore more than 2km of tunnels beneath the streets of Montparnasse, lined with the bones and skulls of millions of Parisians (www.catacombes.paris.fr).

➡ Cimetière Père-Lachaise
Oscar Wilde, Edith Piaf and Jim Morrison are just a few of the famous names buried in this wildly overgrown cemetery (www.perelachaise.com).

➡ Canal St-Martin
Join the locals for a walk or bike ride along the tow-paths of this 4.5km canal, once derelict but now reborn as a haven from the city hustle.

Above Promenade des Anglais (p91); **Right** Cours Saleya, Vieux Nice (p90)

NICE

The classic metropolis of the French Riviera, Nice has something to suit all moods: exceptional museums, atmospheric street markets, glittering Mediterranean beaches and a rabbit-warren old town, all bathed in radiant year-round sunshine. With its blend of city grit and old-world opulence, it deserves as much time as you can spare.

Getting Around

The complicated one-way system and heavy traffic can make driving in Nice stressful, especially in the heat of summer. Walking is the easiest way to get around. There's a handy tram line from the train station all the way to Vieux Nice and place Garibaldi; tickets cost €1.50 and are valid on buses.

Parking

Nearly all parking in Nice is *payant* (chargeable) – assuming you manage to find a space. Car parks are usually cheapest (around €2 to €3 per hour, or €17 to €30 per day). All parking meters take coins; car-park pay stations also accept credit cards.

Where to Eat

Head for the alleyways of Vieux Nice (Old Nice) for the most authentic neighbourhood restaurants. Don't miss the local specialities of *socca* (chickpeaflour pancake), *petitsfarcis* (stuffed vegetables) and *pissaladière* (onion tart topped with black olives and anchovies).

TOP EXPERIENCES

➡ **Strolling the Promenade des Anglais**
Join sun worshippers, inline skaters and dog walkers on this magnificent boulevard, which runs along Nice's shimmering seafront.

➡ **Musée Matisse**
Just 2km north of the centre, this excellent art museum documents the life and work of Henri Matisse in painstaking detail. You'll need good French to get the most out of your visit (www.musee-matisse -nice.org).

➡ **Shopping on Cours Saleya**
This massive market captures the essence of Niçois life. A chaotic assortment of stalls sell everything from fresh-cut flowers to fresh fish.

➡ **Parc du Château**
Pack a picnic and head to this hilltop park for a panorama across Nice's red-tiled rooftops.

Where to Stay
Old town equals atmosphere, but for the best views and classiest rooms you'll want to base yourself near the seafront – the Promenade des Anglais has several landmark hotels. The city's cheapest hotels are clustered around the train station.

Useful Websites
Nice Tourisme (http:// en.nicetourisme.com) Informative city website with info on accommodation and attractions.

Trips Through Nice 3

Destination coverage p90

NEED TO KNOW

CURRENCY
Euro (€)

LANGUAGE
French

VISAS
Generally not required for stays of up to 90 days (or at all for EU nationals); some nationalities need a Schengen visa.

FUEL
Petrol stations are common around main roads and larger towns. Unleaded costs from around €1.60 per litre; *gazole* (diesel) is usually at least €0.15 cheaper.

RENTAL CARS
ADA (www.ada.fr)

Auto Europe (www. autoeurope.com)

Avis (www.avis.com)

Europcar (www.europcar. com)

Hertz (www.hertz.com)

IMPORTANT NUMBERS
Ambulance (☏15)

Police (☏17)

Fire brigade (☏18)

Europe-wide emergency (☏112)

Climate

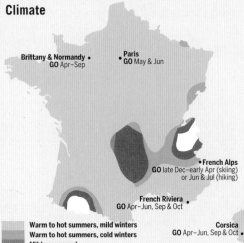

Brittany & Normandy •
GO Apr–Sep

Paris
GO May & Jun

French Alps
GO late Dec–early Apr (skiing) or Jun & Jul (hiking)

French Riviera
GO Apr–Jun, Sep & Oct

Corsica
GO Apr–Jun, Sep & Oct •

- Warm to hot summers, mild winters
- Warm to hot summers, cold winters
- Mild year-round
- Mild summers, cold winters
- Alpine climate

When to Go

High Season (Jul & Aug)
» The main holiday season in France – expect traffic jams and big queues, especially in August.

» Christmas, New Year and Easter are also busy times to travel.

» Late December to March is high season in French ski resorts.

Shoulder Season (Apr–Jun & Sep)
» Balmy temperatures, settled weather and light crowds make this an ideal time to travel.

» Hotel rates drop in busy areas such as southern France and the Atlantic coast.

» The *vendange* (grape harvest) happens in early autumn.

Low Season (Oct–Mar)
» Expect heavy discounts on accommodation (sometimes as much as 50%).

» Snow covers the Alps and Pyrenees, as well as much of central France.

» Many sights and hotels close down for winter.

Daily Costs

Budget: Less than €100
» Double room in a budget hotel: €50–70

» Set lunchtime *menus*: €10–15

Midrange: €100–200
» Double room in a midrange hotel: €70–120

» À la carte mains: €15–20

Top End: Over €200
» Luxury hotel room: €150–200

» Top-end restaurant meal: *menus* from €50, à la carte from €80

Eating

Cafes Coffee, drinks and bar snacks.

Bistros Serve anything from light meals to sit-down dinners.

Restaurants Range from simple *auberges* (country inns) to Michelin-starred wonders.

Vegetarians Limited choice on most menus; look out for *restaurants bios* in cities.

In this book, price symbols indicate the cost of a two-course set menu:

€	under €20
€€	€20–40
€€€	more than €40

Sleeping

Hotels France has a wide range of hotels, from budget to luxury. Unless indicated otherwise, breakfast is extra.

Chambres d'hôte The French equivalent of a B&B; prices nearly always include breakfast.

Hostels Most large towns have a hostel operated by the FUAJ (Fédération Unie des Auberges de Jeunesse).

Price symbols indicate the cost of a double room with private bathroom in high season unless otherwise noted:

€	under €90
€€	€90–190
€€€	more than €190

Arriving in France

Aéroport Roissy Charles de Gaulle (Paris)
Rental cars Major car-rental agencies have concessions at arrival terminals.

Trains, buses and RER
To Paris centre every 15 to 30 minutes, 5am to 11pm.

Taxis €50 to €60; 30 minutes to Paris centre.

Aéroport d'Orly (Paris)
Rental cars Desks beside the arrivals area.

Orlyval rail, RER and buses At least every 15 minutes, 5am to 11pm.

Taxis €45 to €60; 25 minutes to Paris centre.

Mobile Phones

Most European and Australian phones work, but turn off roaming to avoid heavy data charges. Buying a French SIM card provides much cheaper call rates.

Internet Access

Wi-fi is available in most hotels and B&Bs (usually free, but sometimes for a small charge). Many cafes and restaurants also offer free wi-fi to customers.

Money

ATMs are available everywhere. Most major credit cards are accepted (with the exception of American Express). Larger cities have *bureaux de change* (exchange bureaus).

Tipping

By law, restaurant and bar prices are *service compris* (include a 15% service charge). Taxis expect around 10%; round up bar bills to the nearest euro.

Useful Websites

France Guide (www.franceguide.com) Official website run by the French tourist office.

Lonely Planet (www.lonelyplanet.com/france) Travel tips, accommodation, forum and more.

Mappy (www.mappy.fr) Online tools for mapping and journey planning.

France Meteo (www.meteo.fr) The lowdown on the French weather.

About France (www.about-france.com/travel.htm) Tips for driving in France.

> For more, see Road Trip Essentials (p106)

Road Trips

Roman ruins, Site Archéologique de Glanum (p23)
TRABANTOS / SHUTTERSTOCK ©

Roman Provence

Survey Provence's incredible Roman legacy as you follow ancient routes through the region's river gorges and vineyards, gathering provisions as you go.

1

TRIP HIGHLIGHTS

30 km

Pont du Gard
Aqueduct of dizzying scale, magnificently sited

Vaison-la-Romaine

FINISH

5

175 km

Orange
A soaring stage conjures up Rome's splendour

2

START
Nîmes
1

Glanum

3

95 km

Arles
An amphitheatre, Roman market square and underground galleries

Nîmes
A dramatic amphitheatre and an ancient temple

0 km

3 DAYS
205KM / 127 MILES

GREAT FOR...

BEST TIME TO GO
Ruins open year-round, but avoid August's heat and crush.

ESSENTIAL PHOTO

The Pont du Gard, illuminated every night in summer.

BEST FOR CULTURE

Balmy nights at Orange's Théâtre Antique are magic; July includes the Chorégies d'Orange.

1 Roman Provence

Provence was where Rome first truly flexed its imperial muscles. Follow Roman roads, cross Roman bridges and grab a seat in the bleachers at Roman theatres and arenas. You'll discover that most of Provence's Roman ruins aren't ruins at all. Many are exceptionally well preserved, and some are also evocatively integrated into the modern city. With Provence's knockout landscape as a backdrop, history never looked so good!

TRIP HIGHLIGHT

❶ Nîmes (p52)

Although Nîmes isn't strictly speaking in modern Provence, a long, shared regional history means it has to feature in this Roman tour. The city's bizarre coat of arms – a crocodile chained to a palm tree! – recalls the region's first, but definitely not last, horde of sun-worshipping retirees. Julius Caesar's loyal legionnaires were granted land here to settle after hard years

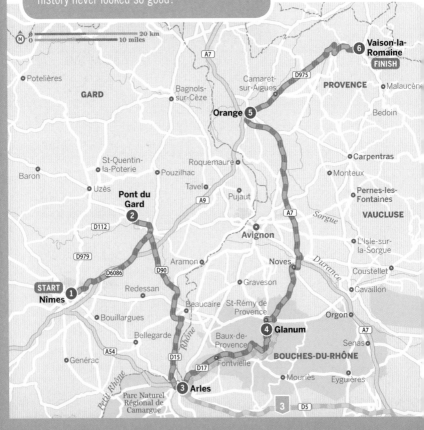

on the Nile campaigns. Two millennia later, their ambitious town blends seamlessly with the bustling, workaday French streetscapes of the modern city. **Les Arènes** (☎04 66 21 82 56; www.arenes-nimes.com; place des Arènes; adult/child incl audioguide €10/8; ☺9am-8pm Jul & Aug, to 6.30pm Apr-Jun & Sep, to 6pm Mar & Oct, 9.30am-5pm Jan, Feb, Nov & Dec), an impressively intact 1st-century-AD amphitheatre, makes for a majestic traffic roundabout. Locals nonchalantly skateboard or window-shop on the elegant place that's home to a beautiful and preciously intact 1st-century-AD temple, the **Maison Carrée** (☎04 66 21 82 56; www.maisoncarree.eu; place de la Maison Carrée; adult/child €6/5; ☺9.30am-8pm Jul & Aug, 10am-6.30pm Apr-Jun & Sep, 10am-6pm Mar & Oct, 10am-1pm & 2-4.30pm Jan, Feb, Nov & Dec). Skip the 22-minute film and instead stroll over to the elegant **Jardins de la Fontaine**. The remains of the **Temple de Diane** are in its lower northwest corner and a 10-minute uphill walk brings you to the crumbling, 30m-high **Tour Magne** (quai de la Fontaine; adult/child €3.50/3, garden free; ☺9am-8pm Jul & Aug, 9am-5pm Sep-Jun). Built in 15 BC as a watchtower and display of imperial grunt, it is the only one that remains of several that once spanned the 7km-long ramparts.

The Drive » From Nîmes it takes 30 minutes on the D6086 and then a short northward leg along the D981 to Pont du Gard.

---

② Pont du Gard (p57)

You'll get a glimpse of the **Pont du Gard** (☎04 66 37 50 99; www.pontdugard.fr; adult/child €8.50/6, Pass Aqueduc incl guided visit of topmost tier €11.50/6; ☺9am-11pm Jul & Aug, to 10pm Jun & Sep, to 9pm May, to 8pm Apr & Oct, to 6pm Nov-Mar) as you approach. Nature (and clever placement of car parks and visitor centres) has created one bravura reveal. Spanning the gorge is a magnificent three-tiered aqueduct, a marvel of 1st-century engineering. During the Roman period, the Pont du Gard was (like Nîmes) part of the Roman province of Gallia Narbonensis. It was built around 19 BC by Agrippa, Augustus' deputy, and it's huge: the 275m-long upper tier, 50m above the Gard, has 35 arches. Each block (the largest weighs over 5 tonnes) was hauled in by cart or raft. It was once part of a 50km-long system that carried water from nearby Uzès down to thirsty Nîmes. It's a 400m wheelchair-accessible walk from car parks on both banks of the river to the bridge itself, with a shady cafe en route on the right. Swim upstream for unencumbered views, though downstream is also good for summer dips, with shaded wooden platforms set in the flatter banks. Want to make a day of it? There's **Museo de la Romanité**, an interactive, information-based museum, plus a children's area, and a peaceful 1.4km botanical walk, **Mémoires de Garrigue**.

The Drive » Kayaking to the next stop would be more fun, and more direct, but you'll need to return south via the D986L

TOP TIP: PADDLING THE GARD RIVER

Get your first glimpse of the Pont du Gard from the river by paddling 8km downstream from Collias, 4km west of the D981. **Kayak Vert** (☎04 66 22 80 76; www.kayakvert.com; 8 chemin de St-Vincent; adult/child from €23/19; ☺9am-6pm mid-May–Oct) and **Canoë Le Tourbillon** (☎04 66 22 85 54; www.canoeletourbillon.com; 3 chemin du Gardon; adult/child from €23/17; ☺9am-7pm Apr-Sep), both based near the village bridge, rent out kayaks and canoes (€20 per person for two hours) from March/April to October.

to Beaucaire, then the D90 and D15 to Arles.

- - - - - - - - - - - - - - - - - - -

TRIP HIGHLIGHT

❸ Arles (p65)

Arles, formerly known as Arelate, was part of the Roman Empire from as early as the 2nd century BC. It wasn't until the 49–45 BC civil war, however, when nearby Massalia (Marseille) supported Pompey (ie backed the wrong side), that it became a booming regional capital.

The town today is delightful, Roman cache or no, but what a living legacy it is. Its **Les Arènes** (Amphithéâtre; ☎08 91 70 03 70; www.arenes-arles. com; Rond-Point des Arènes; adult/child €6/free, incl Théâtre Antique €9/free; ⊘9am-8pm Jul & Aug, to 7pm May, Jun & Sep, shorter hours Oct-Apr) is not as large as Nîmes', but it is spectacularly sited and occasionally still sees blood spilled, just like in the old gladiatorial days (it hosts gory bullfights and *courses Camarguaises,* which is the local variation). Likewise, the 1st-century **Théâtre Antique** (☎04 90 49 59 05; rue de la Calade; adult/child, incl entry to Les Arènes, €9/free; ⊘9am-7pm May-Sep, to 6pm Mar, Apr & Oct, 10am-5pm Nov-Feb) is still regularly used for alfresco performances.

Just as social, political and religious life revolved around the forum in Arelate, the busy plane-tree-shaded **place du Forum** buzzes with cafe life today. Sip a pastis here and spot the remains of a 2nd-century temple embedded in the façade of the **Hôtel Nord-Pinus**. Under your feet are **Cryptoportiques** (place de la République; adult/child €4.50/free; ⊘10am-5pm Nov-Feb, 9am-6pm Mar, Apr & Oct, to 7pm May-Sep) – subterranean foundations and buried arcades. Access the underground galleries, 89m long and 59m wide, at the **Hôtel de Ville** (Town Hall).

Emperor Constantin's partly preserved 4th-century private baths, the **Thermes de Constantin** (☎04 90 49 59 05; rue du Grand Prieuré; adult/child €4/free; ⊘9am-7pm May-Sep, to 6pm Mar, Apr & Oct), are a few minutes' stroll away, next to the *quai* (deck). Southwest of the centre is **Les Alyscamps** (av des Alyscamps; adult/child €4.50/free; ⊘9am-7pm May-Sep, shorter hours rest of year), a necropolis founded by the Romans and adopted by Christians in the 4th century. It contains the tombs of martyr St Genest and Arles' first bishops. You may recognise it: Van Gogh and Gauguin both captured the avenues of cypresses on canvas (though only melancholy old Van Gogh painted the empty sarcophagi).

The Drive ›› Take the D17 to Fontvieille, follow the D78F/D27A to Baux-de-Provence, then the D5. This detour takes you past beautiful dry white rocky hills dotted with scrubby pine trees; the trip will still only take around 45 minutes. There's on-site parking at Glanum. If heading into St-Rémy, there's parking by the tourist office (parking Jean-Jaurès) and north of the periphery (parking Général-de-Gaulle).

- - - - - - - - - - - - - - - - - - -

❹ Glanum (p77)

Such is the glittering allure of the gourmet delis, interiors boutiques and smart restaurants that line St-Rémy-de-Provence's circling boulevards and place de la République that a visit to

S F/SHUTTERSTOCK ©

Les Arènes, Arles

the **Site Archéologique de Glanum** (📞 04 90 92 23 79; www.site-glanum.fr; rte des Baux-de-Provence; adult/child €7.50/free, parking €2.70; ⏰ 9.30am-6.30pm Apr-Sep, 10am-5pm Oct-Mar, closed Mon Sep-Mar) is often an afterthought. But the **triumphal arch** (AD 20) that marks Glanum's entrance, 2km south of St-Rémy, is far from insignificant. It's pegged as one of France's oldest and is joined by a towering **mausoleum** (30–20 BC). Walk down the main street and you'll pass the mainstays of Roman life: baths, a forum and marketplace, temples and town villas. And beneath all this Roman handiwork lies the remnants of an older Celtic and Hellenic settlement, built to take advantage of a sacred spring. Van Gogh, as a patient of the neighbouring asylum, painted the olive orchard that covered the site until its excavation in the 1920s.

The Drive » It's the A7 all the way to Orange, 50km of nondescript driving if you're not

ROMAN PROVENCE READING LIST

» *The Roman Provence Guide* (Edwin Mullins; 2012)

» *The Roman Remains of Southern France* (James Bromwich; 1993)

» *Southern France: An Oxford Archaeological Guide* (Henry Cleere; 2001)

» *Ancient Provence: Layers of History in Southern France* (Jeffrey Wolin; 2003)

SALVE, PROVINCIA GALLIA TRANSALPINA

It all starts with the Greeks. After founding the city of Massalia, now Marseille, around 600 BC, they spent the next few centuries establishing a long string of ports along the coast, planting olives and grapes as they went. When migrating Celts from the north joined forces with the local Ligurians, resistance to these booming colonies grew. The Celto-Ligurians were a force to be reckoned with; unfortunately, they were about to meet ancient history's biggest bullies. In 125 BC the Romans helped the Greeks defend Massalia, and swiftly took control.

Thus began the Gallo-Roman era and the region of Provincia Gallia Transalpina, the first Roman *provincia* (province), the name from which Provence takes it name. Later Provincia Narbonensis, it embraced all of southern France from the Alps to the Mediterranean and the Pyrenees.

Roads made the work of empire possible, and the Romans quickly set about securing a route that joined Italy and Spain. Via Aurelia linked Rome to Fréjus, Aix-en-Provence, Arles and Nîmes; the northbound Via Agrippa followed the Rhône from Arles to Avignon, Orange and onwards to Lyon. The Via Domitia linked the Alps with the Pyrenees by way of the Luberon and Nîmes.

With Julius Caesar's conquest of Gaul (58–51 BC), the region truly flourished. Under the emperor Augustus, vast amphitheatres, triumphal arches and ingenious aqueducts – the ones that propel this trip – were constructed. Augustus celebrated his final defeat of the ever-rebellious Ligurians in 14 BC, with the construction of the monument at La Turbie on the Côte d'Azur.

The Gallo-Roman legacy may be writ large and loud in Provence, but it also persists in the everyday. Look for it in unusual places: recycled into cathedral floors or hotel facades, in dusty cellars or simply buried beneath your feet.

---

tempted by a detour to Avignon on the way.

- - - - - - - - - - - - - - - - - - -

TRIP HIGHLIGHT

❺ Orange (p79)

It's often said if you can only see one Roman site in France, make it Orange. And yes, the town's Roman treasures are gobsmacking and unusually old; both are believed to have been built during Augustus Caesar's rule (27 BC–AD 14). Plus, while Orange may not be the Provençal village of popular fantasy, it's a cruisy, decidedly untouristy town, making for good-value accom-

modation and hassle-free sightseeing (such as plentiful street parking one block back from the theatre).

At a massive 103m wide and 37m high, the stage wall of the **Théâtre Antique** (Ancient Roman Theatre; ☎04 90 51 17 60; www.theatre-antique.com; rue Madeleine Roch; adult/child €9.50/7.50; ⏱9am-7pm Jun-Aug, to 6pm Apr, May & Sep, 9.30am-5.30pm Mar & Oct, 9.30am-4.30pm Nov-Feb) dominates the surrounding streetscape. Minus a few mosaics, plus a new roof, it's one of three in the world still standing in their entirety, and

originally seated 10,000 spectators. Admission includes an informative audioguide, and access to the **Musée d'Art et d'Histoire** (www.theatre-antique.com; rue Madeleine Roch; ⏱9.15am-7pm Jun-Aug, to 6pm Apr, May & Sep, shorter hours Oct-Mar) across the road. Its collection includes friezes from the theatre with the Roman motifs we love: eagles holding garlands of bay leaves, and a cracking battle between cavalrymen and foot soldiers. Note that a major restoration project is currently underway to restore the theatre's limestone structure, which is degrading badly – so unfortunately some scaffolding will be inevitable until at least 2024.

For bird's-eye views of the theatre – and phenomenal vistas of rocky Mont Ventoux and the Dentelles – follow montée Philbert de Chalons, or montée Lambert, up **Colline St-Eutrope**, once the ever-vigilant Romans' lookout point.

To the town's north, the **Arc de Triomphe** stands on the ancient Via Agrippa (now the busy N7), 19m high and wide, and a stonking 8m thick. Restored in 2009, its richly animated reliefs commemorate 49 BC Roman victories with images of battles, ships, trophies, and chained, naked and utterly subdued Gauls.

The Drive » Northeast, the D975 passes through gentle vineyard-lined valleys for 40 minutes, with views of the Dentelles de Montmirail's limestone ridges along the way (the D977 and D23 can be equally lovely). Parking in Vaison can be a trial; park by the tourist office (place du Chanoine Saute), or below the western walls of the Cité Médiévale, if you don't mind walking.

- - - - - - - - - - - - - - - -

⑥ Vaison-la-Romaine (p81)

Is there anything more telling of Rome's smarts than a sturdy, still-used Roman bridge? Vaison-la-Romaine's pretty little **Pont Romain** has stood the test of time and severe floods. Stand at its centre and gaze up at the walled, cobbled-street hilltop **Cité Médiévale**, or down at the fast-flowing Ouvèze River.

Vaison-la-Romaine is tucked between seven valleys and has long been a place of trade. The ruined remains of **Vasio Vocontiorum**, the Roman city that flourished here between around 100 BC and 450 AD, fill two central **Gallo-Roman sites** (☎04 90 36 50 48; www.provenceromaine.com; adult/child incl all ancient sites, museum & cathedral €8/4; ⊙9.30am-6.30pm Jun-Sep, to 6pm Apr & May, 10am-noon & 2-5.30pm Oct-Mar). Dual neighbourhoods lie on either side of the tourist office and av du Général-de-Gaulle. The Romans shopped at the colonnaded boutiques and bathed at **La Villasse**, where you'll find **Maison au Dauphin**, which has splendid marble-lined fish ponds.

In **Puymin**, see noblemen's houses, mosaics, a workmen's quarter, a temple, and the still-functioning 6000-seat **Théâtre Antique** (c AD 20). To make sense of the remains (and gather your audioguide), head for the **archaeological museum**, which revives Vaison's Roman past with an incredible swag: superb mosaics, carved masks, and statues that include a 3rd-century silver bust and marble renderings of Hadrian and his wife, Sabina. Admission includes entry to the soothing 12th-century Romanesque cloister at **Cathédrale Notre-Dame de Nazareth** (cloister only €1.50; ⊙10am-12.30pm & 2-6pm Mar-Dec), a five-minute walk west of La Villasse and, like much of Provence, built on Roman foundations.

Lavender Route

2

Banish thoughts of grandma's closet. Get out among the purple haze, sniff the heady summer breezes and navigate picturesque hilltop towns, ancient churches and pretty valleys.

TRIP HIGHLIGHTS

4–5 DAYS
217KM / 135 MILES

11 km

Abbaye Notre-Dame de Sénanque
Dreamy 12th-century abbey framed by rows of lavender

60 km

Sault
Stop off for wonderful sweets and nougat at confectioner André Boyer

Banon

④

Forcalquier

⑧

② **Gordes**

FINISH
Plateau de Valensole

① **START**

Monosque

Coustellet
Rolling lavender fields and a lavender-themed museum

Prieuré de Salagon
Wander round a medieval herb garden

0 km

165 km

GREAT FOR...

BEST TIME TO GO
July is purple prime time, but June's blooms still impress.

ESSENTIAL PHOTO
The road just north of Sault is a particularly stunning spot.

BEST FOR OUTDOORS
Mont Ventoux has brilliant hiking trails and is hallowed ground for cycling fans.

2 Lavender Route

The Luberon and Vaucluse may be well-trodden (and driven) destinations, but you'll be surprised at how rustic they remain. This trip takes you to the undoubtedly big-ticket (and exquisitely beautiful) sights but also gets you exploring back roads, sleepy villages, big skies and one stunner of a mountain. And yes, past fields and fields of glorious purple blooms.

TRIP HIGHLIGHT

❶ Coustellet

Our lavender trail begins just outside the village of Coustellet at the **Musée de la Lavande** (☎04 90 76 91 23; www.museedelalavande. com; D2; adult/child €6.80/free; ⏱9am-7pm May-Sep, 9am-noon & 2-6pm Oct-Apr), an excellent eco-museum and working lavender farm, where you can take a guided tour of the lavender fields, learn about extraction methods and buy lavender goodies in the on-site boutique.

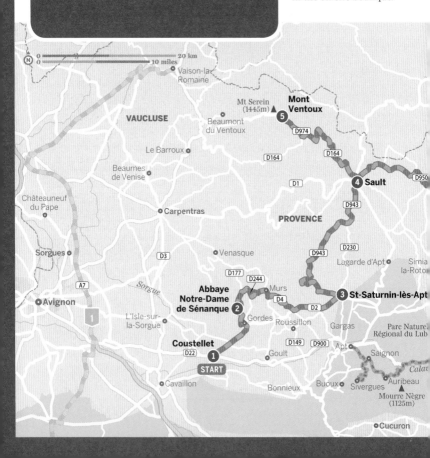

Afterwards the hilltop village of Gordes is worth a detour, especially at sunset, followed perhaps by a drink at the super-swanky **Bastide de Gordes** (📞04 90 72 12 12; www.bastide-de-gordes. com; Le Village; r from €290; ✿🌐⛄) hotel.

The Drive » The museum is just off the D2. From here, it's another 7km to Gordes along the D2, then a turn-off onto the D177 for 4km till you reach the abbey. You'll pass plenty of lavender photo ops en route, so feel free to stop if you can find an appropriate spot.

TRIP HIGHLIGHT

❷ Abbaye Notre-Dame de Sénanque (p85)

Isolated and ridiculously photogenic, this 12th-century Cistercian **abbey** (📞04 90 72 05 72; www.ab bayedesenanque.com; adult/ child €7.50/3.50; ⏰9-11.30am Mon-Sat Apr-Nov, shorter hours Dec-Mar) is famously framed by lavender from mid-June through July. The abbey was founded in 1148 and is still home to a small number of monks. The cloisters

have a haunting, severe beauty; reservations are essential to visit inside, but out of high season they can be made on-site (conservative dress and silence are required). Tours begin around 10am, so for some tranquil time with the lavender, arrive well before then.

The Drive » The way out of the abbey has you heading north. Continue up the D177 then turn right onto the D244 and follow the signs to Murs, a very winding 9.5km drive accompanied by wheat fields and vineyards. From here it's about 25 minutes to the next stop.

❸ St-Saturnin-lès-Apt (p87)

St-Saturnin-lès-Apt is a refreshingly ungentrified village, with marvellous views of the surrounding Vaucluse plateau punctuated by purple fields – climb to the **ruins** atop the village for a knockout vista. At **Moulin à Huile Jullien** (📞04 90 75 56 24; www.moulin-huile-jullien.com;

LINK YOUR TRIP

1 Roman Provence
From Roman Provence's last stop in Vaison-la-Romaine, it's a gorgeous drive to Coustellet via Carpentras and Venasque.

PHB.CZ (RICHARD SEMIK)/SHUTTERSTOCK ©

rte d'Apt; ⏰10am-noon & 3-7pm Jul & Aug, 10am-noon & 2-6pm Sep-Jun, closed Sun year-round) see how olives are milled into oil (with honey and oil tastings thrown in). You'll see huge lavender fields as you drive past the **Château du Bois**, 20km to the northeast, the same estate that runs the shop and lavender museum in Coustellet.

The Drive ≫ Spot the pretty 17th-century windmill, Le Château les Moulins, 1km north, off the D943 towards Sault, then look out for the magnificent views of the red-tinged escarpment and the rust-coloured village of Roussillon. The views of Mont Ventoux only get more spectacular as you approach Sault, a 35-minute drive away.

- - - - - - - - - - - - - - - -

TRIP HIGHLIGHT

❹ Sault

This drowsily charming, isolated hilltop town mixes its lavender views with plum orchards and scattered forest. The town hot spot is **André**

Boyer (☎04 90 64 00 23; www.nougat-boyer.fr; place de l'Europe), which has kept farmers, cyclists and mountaineers in honey and almond nougat since 1887; its lavender marsh-mallows and the local speciality *pognes* (an orange-scented brioche) are also must-tries. Head to **GAEC Champelle** (☎04 90 64 01 50; www.gaec-champelle.fr; rte de Ventoux), a roadside farm stand northwest of town, whose products include great buys for cooks. The lavender up here is known for its dark, OK... deep purple, hue.

The Drive ≫ Exit town on the D164; when you hit the D974, fields give way to dense, fragrant forest. Above the treeline, strange spots of alpine scrub are gradually replaced by pale bald slopes. These steep gradients have often formed a hair-raising stage of the Tour de France – the road is daubed with Tour graffiti and many fans make a brave two-wheeled homage.

- - - - - - - - - - - - - - - -

❺ Mont Ventoux (p82)

If fields of flowers are in-toxicating, Mont Ventoux (1912m) is awe-inspiring. Nicknamed *le géant de Provence* – Provence's giant – its great white hulk is visible from much of the region. *Le géant* sparkles all year round – once the snow melts, its lunar-style limestone slopes glimmer in the sun. From its peak, clear-day vistas extend to the Alps and the Camargue.

Even summer tem-peratures can plummet by 20°C at the top; it's also twice as likely to

**TOP TIP:
LAVENDER: FINDING
THE GOOD OIL**

When shopping for oil, the sought-after product is fine lavender (in French, *lavande fine;* in Latin, *L. officinalis*), not spike lavender (*L. latifolia*) or the hybrid lavandin (*Lavandula x intermedia*). The latter are higher in camphor; they're used in soaps and body-care products but rarely in fine perfumery. They're also used to adulterate true lavender oil. Look for oil that's clearly labelled and lacks a harsh camphor note.

Forcalquier

rain; and the relentless mistrals blow 130 days a year, sometimes exceeding 250km/h. Bring a cardigan and scarf!

The Drive » Go back the way you came to Sault, then head east to Banon on the D950 for another 40 minutes.

---

6 Banon

A tasty, nonfloral diversion: little village, big cheese. Bustling Banon is famous for its chèvre de Banon, a goat's-milk cheese wrapped in a chestnut leaf. Fromagerie de Banon sells its cheese at the Tuesday morning market, and at wonder-

ful cheese-and-sausage shop **Brindille Melchio** (☏04 92 73 23 05; place de la République; ⏰8am-12.30pm & 2.30-6.30pm Wed-Sun Sep-Jun, 8am-7pm daily Jul & Aug), which is unbeatable for picnic supplies. Tuck into cheese-and-charcuterie plates at **Les Vins au Vert** (☏04 92 75 23 84; https:// restaurant-caviste-banon-04.fr; rue Pasteur; menus €13.50-15; ⏰10am-3pm & 5.30-11pm Thu-Sat, to 3pm Wed & Sun); make reservations for Thursday to Saturday nights.

The Drive » Follow the D950 southeast for 25km to Forcalquier, as the scenery alternates between gentle forested slopes and fields.

---

7 Forcalquier (p88)

Forcalquier has an upbeat, slightly bohemian vibe, a holdover from the 1960s and '70s, when artists and back-to-the-landers arrived, fostering a now-booming organics (*'biologiques'* or bio) movement. Saffron is grown here, absinthe is distilled, and the town is also home to L'Université Européenne des Senteurs & Saveurs (UESS; European University of Scents and Flavours). To see it all in action, time your visit for the Monday morning market.

Climb the steep steps to Forcalquier's gold-topped **citadel** and octagonal **chapel** for more sensational views; on the way down note the once-wealthy seat's ornately carved wooden doorways and grand bourgeois town houses. Pop in for a drink, a Michelin-starred meal and (if budget allows) an overnight stay at the luxurious **Couvent des Minimes** ([📞]04 92 74 77 77; www.couventdesminimes -hotelspa.com; chemin des Jeux de Maï, Mane; r from €310; [❄][📶][🏊]), owned by fragrance house L'Occitane.

The Drive » Find yourself in a gentle world, all plane-tree arcades, wildflowers and, yes,

lavender. Around 4km south on the D4100 you'll come to our next stop, just before the pretty town of Mane.

TRIP HIGHLIGHT

8 Prieuré de Salagon (p88)

This beautiful 13th-century priory, located on the outskirts of Mane, is today home to a garden museum, the **Jardins Salagon** ([📞]04 92 75 70 50; www.musee-de-salagon.com; adult/child €8/6; [🕐]10am-8pm Jun-Aug, to 7pm May & Sep, to 6pm Oct–mid-Dec & Feb-Apr; [♿]). This is ethno-botany at its most poetic and sensual: wander through recreated medieval herb gardens, fragrant with

native lavender, mints and mugworts. The bookshop is inviting, too.

The walled town of **Mane** is lovely for strolling. Or for a mysterious, potentially curative detour, visit remote **Église de Châteauneuf**, where a hermit church sister concocts natural remedies and makes jam. Head 800m south of Mane to the Hôtel Mas du Pont Roman, then turn right and either park and walk, or drive the bumpy final 3km. Be warned: the good sister doesn't always reveal herself. Just in case, bring a picnic and consider it an adventure.

The Drive » Get on the D13, then follow the signs to the D5 for the drive to Manosque (roughly 30 minutes in total).

----

9 Manosque

Manosque has two lovely fountains and a historic cobblestoned core, but the traffic and suburban nothingness make visiting a nuisance. Why swing by? Just southeast is the home of **L'Occitane** (https://fr.loccitane.com; Zone Industrielle St-Maurice; [🕐]10am-7pm Mon-Sat), the company that turned traditional lavender-, almond- and olive oil–based Provençal skincare into a global phenomenon. Factory tours can be booked through the **tourist office** ([📞]04 92 72 16 000); the shop offers a

DETOUR: THE LUBERON

Start: 8 Prieuré de Salagon

The Luberon's other, southern, half is equally florally blessed. Lavender carpets the **Plateau de Claparèdes** between **Buoux** (west), **Sivergues** (south), **Auribeau** (east) and **Saignon** (north). Cycle, walk or motor through the lavender fields and along the northern slopes of **Mourre Nègre** (1125m) – the Luberon's highest point, accessible from **Auribeau**. The D113 climbs to idyllic lavender distillery **Les Agnels** ([📞]04 90 74 34 60; www.lesagnels.com; rte de Buoux, btwn Buoux & Apt; adult/child €6/free; [🕐]10am-7pm Apr-Sep, to 5.30pm Oct-Mar), which distils lavender, cypress and rosemary. The small on-site spa has a lavender-scented swimming pool. Stay at **Chambre avec Vue** ([📞]04 90 04 85 01; www.chambreavecvue.com; rue de la Bourgade; r €90-140; [🕐]closed Dec-Feb) in tiny Saignon, which perches on high rocky flanks, its narrow streets crowning a hill ringed with craggy scrub and petite lavender plots, with incredible vistas across the Luberon to Mont Ventoux.

Skin-care company, L'Occitane in Manosque

flat 10% discount and the odd bargain.

The Drive » Leave the freeways and ring roads behind and cross the Durance River towards the quieter D6 (from where it will take around 20 minutes to reach the town of Valensole); make sure you check the rear-view mirrors for mountain views to the northwest as you do.

 Plateau de Valensole (p88)

Things get very relaxed once you hit the D6, and the road begins a gentle climb. Picnic provisions packed, wind down your windows.

This dreamily quiet plateau has Provence's greatest concentration of lavender farms, and a checkerboard of waving wheat and lavender rows stretch to the horizon, or at least to Riez. Fine picnic spots and photo ops are not hard to find.

✓ TOP TIP: BEST PRODUCE MARKETS

The Luberon has groaning markets run from 8am to 1pm; they're particularly thrilling in summer.

Monday Forcalquier
Tuesday Apt, Gordes, St-Saturnin-lès-Apt
Wednesday Gargas
Thursday Roussillon
Friday Bonnieux, Lourmarin
Saturday Apt, Manosque
Sunday Coustellet, Villars

Modern Art Meander

3

Provence is where many 20th-century artists found their greatest source of inspiration. Cross this photogenic, good-time region and discover its vibrant, creative history along the way.

TRIP HIGHLIGHTS

7 DAYS
340KM / 211 MILES

GREAT FOR...

50 km

Fondation Maeght
Impressive 20th-century collection with equally outstanding sculpture garden

0 km

Musée Jean Cocteau
Unique artist's vision in fascinating contemporary architecture

St-Rémy de Provence
FINISH

Arles

START

3 **2** **1**

Biot
Antibes

8

225 km

Atelier Cézanne
Post-impressionist master's evocative studio

30 km

Musée National Marc Chagall
Exuberant huge oils, stained glass and mosaics

BEST TIME TO GO
Winter – how it used to be done.

ESSENTIAL PHOTO

A snap in the bar of La Colombe d'Or is a nice trophy for art groupies.

BEST TWO DAYS

Concentrate on Picasso on the Cote d'Azur, or combine Van Gogh and Cézanne in Provence proper (Arles, Aix and St-Rémy).

Modern Art Meander

There's a particular kind of magic that happens when you connect with a work of art in the place it was created. This trip includes the region's stellar art museums, but also takes you to the bays, beaches, fields, hilltop eyries, bars and bustling boulevards where the Modern masters lived, worked and partied. And it's all bathed in Provence's glorious, ever-inspirational light.

TRIP HIGHLIGHT

❶ Menton (p104)

Menton is known for two things: lemons and an exceptionally sunny climate. The recent opening of the **Musée Jean Cocteau Collection Séverin Wunderman** (📞04 89 81 52 50; www.museecocteaumenton.fr; 2 quai de Monléon; adult/child Jun-Oct €10/free, Nov-May €8/free; ⏱10am-6pm Wed-Mon) will give Menton a new claim to fame. The artist-poet Jean Cocteau was an honoured adopted son of the town; the collection fo-

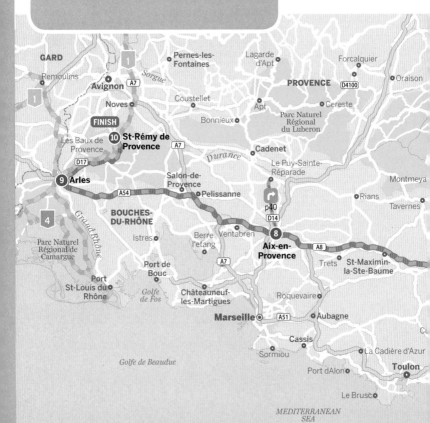

cuses mainly on Cocteau's illustrations, but also includes his poetic, experimental films. You can catch delightful glimpses of palms and sparkling sea from slashes in the skin of Rudy Ricciotti's architecturally ambitious building. Cocteau decorated the local **Salle des Mariages** (Registry Office; ☎04 92 10 50 00; www.menton.fr/La-Salle-des-Mariages.html; place Ardoïno; adult/child €2/free; ⏰8.30am-noon & 2-4.30pm Mon-Fri) in 1957, and don't miss his rendering of France's official mascot, Marianne.

The Drive ≫ Take the coast road – the gorgeous basse corniche – for about 45 minutes via Roquebrune St-Martin.

TRIP HIGHLIGHT

❷ Nice (p90)

The Cote d'Azur capital is home to two iconic museums. The **Musée National Marc Chagall** (☎04 93 53 87 20; www.musee-chagall.fr; 4 av Dr Ménard; adult/child €10/8; ⏰10am-6pm Wed-Mon May-Oct, to 5pm Nov-Apr; 🚌15, 22 to Musée Chagall) houses the largest public collection of works by Marc Chagall, including monumental paintings, tapestries and glasswork. It's set in an impressive contemporary space

LINK YOUR TRIP

Roman Provence
1 The 20th-century artists were inspired by this heritage;

join in Arles or St-Rémy (and the sunflower therapy around Nîmes is sweet).

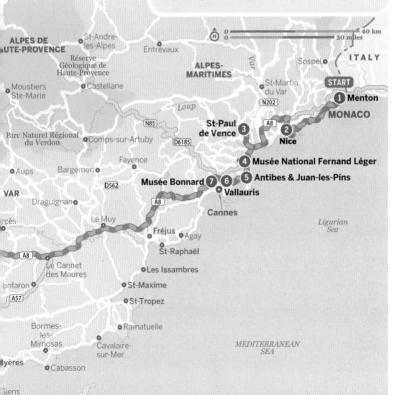

perched high over the city. Up in the leafy quarter of Cimiez, the **Musée Matisse** (📞04 93 81 08 08; www.musee-matisse-nice .org; 164 av des Arènes de Cimiez; museum pass 24hr/7 days €10/20; ⏰10am-6pm Wed-Mon late Jun–mid-Oct, from 11am rest of year; 🚌15, 17, 20, 22 to Arènes/Musée Matisse) overlooks an olive-tree-studded park and Roman ruins. Its beautiful Genoese villa houses a charming, if slightly underwhelming, permanent collection.

Do also make the most of Nice's burgeoning antiques and vintage scene. Browse **rue Delfy** and the streets running from place Garibaldi towards the port. The most serious dealers can be found in **rue Segurane** and the **puce** (flea market; corner rue Robilant and quai Lunel).

The Drive » The coast road between Nice and Cannes is often gridlocked, so jump on the A8 to Cagnes-sur-Mer, about a 15-minute drive, then exit to the D336 to St-Paul de Vence. From here on, the inland run is pretty. Signs to Fondation Maeght appear 500m before the entrance to the village.

TRIP HIGHLIGHT

❸ St-Paul de Vence (p100)

Chagall, Picasso, Soutine, Léger and Cocteau 'discovered' this hilltop medieval village and were joined by the showbiz set, such as Yves Montand and Roger Moore. Chagall is buried in the **cemetery** at the village's southern end (immediately to the right as you enter).

St-Paul's fortified core is beautifully preserved but gets overrun in high summer. Escape to the **pétanque pitch**, just before the entrance to the village proper, where many a tipsy painter or tousled film star has had a spin.

Below the village, the **Fondation Maeght** (📞04 93 32 81 63; www. fondation-maeght.com; 623 chemin des Gardettes; adult/ child €15/10; ⏰10am-7pm Jul-Sep, to 6pm Oct-Jun) has one of the largest private collections of 20th-century art in Europe, in a Sert-designed building that's a masterpiece itself. There's a Giacometti courtyard, sculptures dotted across the deeply terraced gardens, coloured-glass windows by Braque and mosaics by Chagall.

Head north to **Vence** and look for the blue-and-white ceramic roof tiles of Matisse's **Chapelle du Rosaire** (Rosary Chapel; 📞04 93 58 03 26; www.vence.fr/the-rosaire -chapel; 466 av Henri Matisse; adult/child €7/4; ⏰10am-noon & 2-6pm Tue, Thu & Fri, 2-6pm Wed & Sat Apr-Oct, to 5pm Nov-Mar). Inside, an architecturally stark space is dominated by madly playful **stained-glass windows** in glowing blue, yellow and green, while

DIY ART COLLECTION: BROCANTE BROWSING

OK, it's highly unlikely you'll come across an obscure Picasso etching for a song. Those New York decorators and Parisian dealers will have got there first. But the *brocante* (vintage and antique) markets of Provence do continue to turn up interesting midcentury ceramics, paintings and works on paper. Banish the thought of excess baggage: these are trip mementos you'll treasure for life.

Get up early and join the locals (a regular mooch around the *puce* – flea market – is an integral part of French life), as dealers are at their most charming and chatty first thing in the morning. **L'Isle-sur-la-Sorgue** (an hour's drive northwest of Aix-en-Provence) is known for its sprawling stalls, and runs each weekend. Both **Nice** and **Aix-en-Provence** also have weekly meets (Nice's cours Saleya hosts on Monday mornings, Aix's on Tuesday, Thursday and Saturday on place Verdun). **Arles** holds one on the first Wednesday of the month on the bd des Lices.

sketchy, almost brutal, Stations of the Cross are rendered on tile; the artist declared it 'the fruit of my whole working life'.

The Drive » Head back the way you came to Cagnes-sur-Mer, then go south for 10 minutes towards Antibes. The Musée Léger is just inland from the freeway, 2km before Biot. Look out for its brown sign.

St-Paul de Vence

❹ Musée National Fernand Léger

Just below the charming little village of Biot, the **Musée National Fernand Léger** (☎04 92 91 50 20; www.musee-fernandleger. fr; chemin du Val de Pôme; adult/child incl audioguide €5.50/free, special exhibitions additional €2; ⊙10am-6pm Wed-Mon May-Oct, to 5pm Nov-Apr) has an excellent monograph collection that captures Léger's wonderful intellectual curiosity as well as his arresting visual style.

The Drive » Head directly across the coast and then south to Antibes for about 15 minutes.

❺ Antibes & Juan-les-Pins (p102)

Picasso once said that to see his paintings from Antibes, you must go to Antibes.

Picasso and Max Ernst were captivated by this pretty port town (as was a restless Graham Greene). Do as Picasso commanded, and head to the **Musée Picasso** (☎04 92 90

54 26; www.antibes-juanlespins. com/culture/musee-picasso; Château Grimaldi, 4 rue des Cordiers; adult/concession €6/3; ⊙10am-6pm Tue-Sun mid-Jun–mid-Sep, to 1pm & 2-6pm Tue-Sun rest of year) in the 14th-century Château Grimaldi, his studio after WWII. Look for works featuring the serenely beautiful face of Françoise Gilot, Picasso's partner of 10 years (he met Gilot in an Antibes' restaurant).

Park to explore Vieux Antibes, then hop in the car to clock **Hôtel du Cap Eden Roc**. This summer favourite of Hemingway, Picasso and others featured as the thinly disguised, fictional Hôtel des Étrangers in F Scott Fitzgerald's *Tender Is the Night* (1934).

The Drive » Take the D6107 out of Antibes, and connect with the D6007, parallel to the coast, a 20-minute trip.

❻ Vallauris

Picasso discovered this potters' village in 1947, along with his own passion for clay. He produced thousands of works here for the next eight years (many on display at the Musée Picasso in Antibes) as well as his last great political composition, a collection of dramatic murals, now part of the **Musée National Picasso 'La Guerre et la Paix** (☎04 93 64 71 83; www.mu see-picasso-vallauris.fr; place de la Libération; adult/child €5/free; ⊙10am-12.15pm & 2-5pm Wed-Mon Sep-Jun, longer hours Jul & Aug)'. Picasso left Vallauris another gift: a dour bronze, **L'Homme au Mouton**, on place Paul Isnard (adjoining place de la Libération). But his greatest legacy was the revival of the centuries-old local ceramics industry; exuberant

'60s pieces by the likes of Roger Capon are now highly collectable, and the town is today dotted with potteries.

The Drive » The D803 will get you out of Vallauris, then to the Chemin des Collines to Le Cannet, a 6km flit.

❼ Le Musée Bonnard

Pierre Bonnard's luminous, quiet, intensely personal paintings are often overlooked in the fast and furious narrative of the avant-garde. Bonnard had a base in Le Cannet from 1922, and lived here almost continuously during the last decade of his life. The collection at **Musée Bonnard** (📞04 93 94 06 06; www.museebonnard.fr; 16 bd Sadi Carnot, Le Cannet; adult/child €5/3.50; ⏰10am-6pm Tue-Sun Sep-Jun, to 8pm Jul & Aug) includes fascinating early pieces and ephemera, but it's the local light and the colour of the artist's mature works that are truly unforgettable, for fans and new converts alike.

The Drive » Make sure you're fed and fuelled up before hitting the A8 west, with a 1½-hour drive to Aix-en-Provence. Once there, head north on the ring road, eyes peeled for the D14 exit, then veer right into the av Paul Cézanne. Note, the street is steep and there's no marked parking.

DETOUR: CHÂTEAU LA COSTE

Start: ❽ Aix-en-Provence

Hello 21st century! If you're partial to site-specific installation, don't miss **Château la Coste** (📞04 42 61 92 92; www.chateau-la-coste.com; 2750 Route de la Cride, Le Puy Sainte Réparade; art walk adult/child €15/12; ⏰cellar door 9am-7.30pm Mon-Sat, from 10am Sun May-Sep, to 6.30pm Oct-Apr).

Taking a traditional domaine surrounded by wooded hills, Irish property developer Paddy McKillen has created one of the south's most compelling, and idiosyncratic, contemporary-art collections. A 90-minute walk takes you out into the landscape, discovering works by artists such as Andy Goldsworthy, Sean Scully, Tatsuo Miyajima and Richard Serra. In all there are 20 pieces, with more to come. McKillen also has chosen a roll-call of starchitects to design the modern structures: a 'floating' gallery/visitors centre is by Tadeo Ando, and the cellars by Jean Nouvel. Book ahead for a guided cellar visit.

If you don't have time for the hike, taste excellent organic whites, reds and rosés in the shop, and lunch at the casual restaurant between a Louise Bourgeois spider and an Alexander Calder – bliss!

From Aix, take the D14 north. The road splits after 10km, but stay on the D14, which becomes a flawless country drive. Château la Coste is well signposted from there.

TRIP HIGHLIGHT

❽ Aix-en-Provence (p59)

Oil renderings by post-impressionist Paul Cézanne of the hinterland of his hometown are forcefully beautiful and profoundly revolutionary, their use of geometric layering to create depth making way for the abstract age to come. For art lovers, Aix is hallowed ground.

The painter's last studio, **Atelier Cézanne** (📞04 42 21 06 53; www.atelier-cezanne.com; 9 av Paul Cézanne; adult/child €6.50/free, audioguide €3; ⏰10am-6pm Jun-Sep, 10am-12.30pm & 2-6pm Apr & May, 10.30am-12.30pm & 2-5pm Oct-Mar, closed Sun Dec-Feb; 🚌5, 12), 1.5km north of town, has been painstakingly preserved. The painterly clutter is set-dressed, yes, but it's still a sublimely evocative space with soaring iron windows and sage walls washed with a patina of age. Further up the hill **Terrain des Peintres** (www. terrain-des-peintres-aix -en-provence.fr; chemin de la Marguerite; 🚌5, 12) is a wonderful terraced garden from where Cézanne, among others, painted Montagne Ste-Victoire.

Visits to his other two sites must be booked ahead on the official **tourism website** (www. aixenprovencetourism. com): **Bastide du Jas de Bouffan** (☎04 42 16 11 61; www.cezanne-en-provence. com; 17 route de Galice; adult/ child €6/free; ⊙ guided tours from 10.30am daily Jun-Sep, Tue, Thu & Sat May & Oct, Wed & Sat Nov-Mar), his country manor west of the centre, and his rented cabin at **Carrières de Bibémus** (Bibémus Quarries; ☎04 42 16 11 61; www.cezanne-en -provence.com; 3090 chemin de Bibémus; adult/child €7.70/ free; ⊙ English-language tours 11am Apr, May & Oct; 🅿), by a quarry on the edge of town. The latter is where he produced most of his sublime Montagne Ste-Victoire paintings.

The city's excellent **Musée Granet** (☎04 42 52 88 32; www.museegranet -aixenprovence.fr; place St-Jean de Malte; adult/child €5.50/ free; ⊙10am-7pm Tue-Sun mid-Jun–Sep, noon-6pm Tue-Sun Oct–mid-Jun) has nine of Cézanne's paintings, though often not on display at the same time (ironically, back in the day, the then director

TOP TIP:
JEAN COCTEAU TRAIL

The dreamy work of Jean Cocteau makes a wonderful mini-trip itinerary. See his murals at Villa Santo Sospir, and discover more of his Cote d'Azur legacy on the **Route Jean Cocteau** (www.le-sud-jean-cocteau.org).

turned down donations by the painter himself).

The Drive » For this one-hour drive, start by getting back onto the A8 and head towards Salon-de-Provence; just before the town, take the A54 (aka E80) to Arles. Note that the N113 merges with this road from St-Martin-de-Crau.

⑨ Arles (p65)

Let's get this out of the way: though he painted 200-odd canvases in Arles, there are no Vincent Van Goghs to see. Instead, come to retrace the streetscapes that fill his bursting canvases, like the **cafe** from *Café Terrace at Night* (1888), which still sits on the place du Forum. Pick up a detailed Van Gogh walking map from the tourist office.

Arles today has an enduring creative vibe and a booming art and artisan scene, concentrated southwest of place du Forum and towards the *quai*. It's also host to an exciting international photography festival, **Les Rencontres d'Arles Photographie** (www. rencontres-arles.com)

running from early July to September.

The Drive » From Arles head to the D17. This is a 45-minute direct drive, but the Alpilles landscape is one worth slowing down for. Join the D5 after 20km or so, then the Monastère St-Paul de Mausole is 2km before town.

⑩ St-Rémy de Provence

St-Rémy might be chic, but like Arles, it hasn't got a Van Gogh. A couple of kilometres south of the town, though, the **Monastère St-Paul de Mausole** (☎04 90 92 77 00; www.saintpauldemausole. fr; adult/child €5/free; ⊙9.30am-6.45pm Apr-Sep, 10.15am-5.15pm Oct-Mar, closed Jan–mid-Feb) is a tranquil, if terribly poignant, part of the Van Gogh story. The painter admitted himself to the asylum here in 1889, and his stay proved to be one of his most productive periods (it was here that he painted his irises). View a reconstruction of his room and stroll the gardens and Romanesque cloister that feature in several of his works.

The Camargue

Take this semicircular tour from Arles to the coast and loop back to experience Provence at its most wild, lush and lovely. Welcome to a watery, dreamlike landscape like no other.

4

TRIP HIGHLIGHTS

38 km

Stes-Maries-de-la-Mer
A 12th-century church houses the eponymous saints

START/FINISH
① **0 km**

Arles
Home to Provence's hippest square

Étang de Vaccarès ● Le Sambuc

⑤

③

86 km

Salin de Badon
Watch flamingos swoop over wetlands as you walk past

Le Point ● de Vue

⑦

110 km

Plage de Piémanson
End-of-the-earth feel with miles of windswept beach

4 DAYS
190KM / 118 MILES

GREAT FOR...

BEST TIME TO GO

May, July and September – if you can handle heat and mosquitoes.

 ESSENTIAL PHOTO

Le Point de Vue for its salty backdrop and flocks of flamingos taking flight.

☑ **BEST FOR ROMANTICS**

Dinner by the hearth in the timber-beamed 17th-century kitchen of Mas de Peint.

4 The Camargue

Leave Arles and the highway behind and suddenly you're surrounded by the Camargue's great yawning green, and an equally expansive sky. It won't be long until you spot your first field of cantering white horses, or face off with a black bull. This is not a long trip, but one that will plunge you into an utterly unique world of cowboys, fishers, beachcombers, and the Roma and all their enduring traditions.

TRIP HIGHLIGHT

❶ Arles (p65)

Befitting its role as gateway to the Camargue, Arles has a delightfully insouciant side. Long home to bohemians of all stripes, it's a great place to hang up your sightseeing hat for a few languorous hours (or days). Soak it in from the legendary bar at the **Hôtel Nord-Pinus** (☏04 90 93 44 44; www.nord-pinus. com; place du Forum; s/d €232/368; ✳🐾), with its bullfighting trophies and

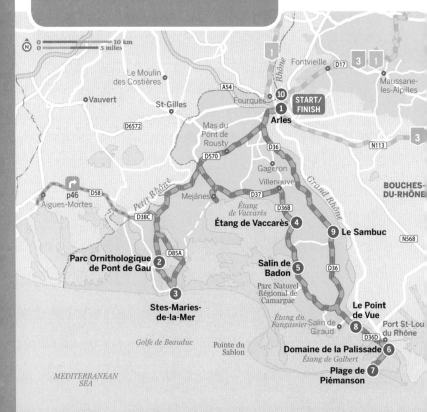

enthralling photography collection, or pull up a table on lively **place Paul Doumer**, where Arles' new generation makes its mark. Make a beeline for the Saturday-morning **market** (bd des Lices) and pack a Camargue-worthy picnic basket with local goat's cheese, olives and *saucisson d'Arles* (bull-meat sausage), or do likewise on Wednesday mornings on bd Émile Combes.

With precious little parking within the old town, unless you're staying at a hotel with a garage (usually an expensive extra), opt for the secure municipal facilities on bd des Lices (€7 per day).

The Drive » Take the D35A across the Grand Rhône at the Pont de Trinquetaille, then follow signs to the D570 – you'll soon be in no doubt you've entered the Camargue. Continue south on the D570 until Pont de Gau, 4km before you hit the coast, around 30 minutes all up.

LINK YOUR TRIP

1 **Roman Provence**
Slot in the Camargue from either Nîmes or Arles.

2 **Lavender Route**
From Arles, take the 570N and the D28 (direction Châteaurenard), then the D900 to Coustellet.

2 Parc Ornithologique de Pont de Gau (p74)

Itching to get in among all that green? **Parc Ornithologique de Pont de Gau** (☎04 90 97 82 62; www.parcornithologique.com; D570, Pont du Gau; adult/child €7.50/5; ☺9am-7pm Apr-Sep, 10am-6pm Oct-Mar; P ⛹), a 60-hectare bird park, makes for a perfect pit stop. As you meander along 7km of trails, flamingos pirouette overhead; the pink birds can't help play diva. Secreted away in the marshes, though, is every bird species that calls the Camargue wetlands home, including herons, storks, egrets, teals and raptors.

The Drive » Continue south on the D570. The last stretch of road into Stes-Maries-de-la-Mer is dotted with stables – little-white-horse heaven, so get out your camera.

TRIP HIGHLIGHT

3 Stes-Maries-de-la-Mer (p74)

Apart from a stretch of fine sand beaches – some 30km – the main attraction at this rough-and-tumble beach resort is the hauntingly beautiful **Église des Stes-Maries** (☎04 90 97 80 25; www.sanctuaire-des-saintesmaries.fr; 2 place de l'Église; rooftop €2.50; ☺10am-noon & 2-5pm Mon-Sat, 2-5pm Sun), a 12th-century church

that's home to a statue of Sara-la-Kali, or black Sara. The crypt houses her alleged remains, along with those of Marie-Salomé and Marie-Jacobé, the Maries of the town's name. Shunned by the Vatican, this paleo-Christian trio has a powerful hold on the Provençal psyche, with a captivating back story involving a boat journey from Palestine and a cameo from Mary Magdalene. Sara is the patron saint of the *gitans* (Roma people), and on 24 and 25 May each year, thousands come to town to pay their respects and party hard. Don't miss the ex-voto paintings that line the smoke-stained walls, personal petitions to Sara that are touching and startlingly strange in turns.

This town is the easiest spot to organise *promenades à cheval* (horseback riding); look for Fédération Française d'Equitation (FFE) accredited places, such as the friendly **Cabanes de Cacharel** (☎04 90 97 84 10, 06 11 57 74 75; www.cabanesdecacharel.com; rte de Cacharel, D85A; horse trek per hour/day €22/70) on the easterly D85A.

The Drive » The scenic D85A rejoins the D570. After 10 minutes or so, turn right onto the D37. Stop at Méjanes for supplies or to visit the legendary fish restaurant Le Mazet du Caccarés. The D36B dramatically skims the eastern lakeshore; it's

GOUM/SHUTTERSTOCK ©

a 20-minute journey but is worth taking your time over.

④ Étang de Vaccarès (p71)

This 600-sq-km lagoon, with its watery labyrinth of peninsulas and islands, is where the wetlands are at their most dense, almost primordial. Much of its tenuous shore forms the **Réserve Nationale de Camargue** and is off-limits, making the wonderful nature trails and wildlife observatories at **La Capelière** (☎04 90 97 00 97; www.reserve-camargue.org; C134, rte de Fiélouse; permits adult/child €3/1.50; ⊙9am-1pm & 2-6pm Apr-Sep, to 5pm Wed-Mon Oct-Mar) particularly precious. The 1.5km-long **Sentier des Rainettes** (Tree-Frog Trail) takes you through tamarisk woodlands and the grasses of brackish open meadows.

The Drive » Continue on the D36B past Fiélouse for around 10 minutes.

TRIP HIGHLIGHT

⑤ Salin de Badon

Before you leave La Capelière, grab your permits for another outstanding reserve site, once the **royal salt works** (adult/child €3/1.50). Around the picturesque ruins are a number of observatories and 4.5km of wild trails – spy on flamingos wading through springtime irises. True birdwatchers mustn't miss a night in the **gîte** (www.snpn.com/reservedecamargue; off the D36B; dm €12) here, a bare-bones cottage in a priceless location.

The Drive » Continue south until you meet the D36, turning right. Stop in Salin de Giraud for bike hire and fuel or visit the salt works. The D36 splits off to cross the Rhône via punt, but you continue south on the

D36D, where it gets exciting: spectacular salt pans appear on your right, the river on your left.

DETOUR: AIGUES-MORTES

Start ③ Stes-Maries-de-la-Mer

Located over the border from Provence in the Gard, Aigues-Mortes sits a winding 28km northwest of Stes-Maries-de-la-Mer at the Camargue's far western extremity. Its central axis of streets often throngs with tourists, but the town is nonetheless magnificent, set in flat marshland and completely enclosed by rectangular ramparts and a series of towers. Come sundown, things change pace, and its squares are a lovely place to join locals for a relaxed *apéro* (pre-dinner drink). Established by Louis IX in the mid-13th century to give the French crown a Mediterranean port, it was from here that the king launched the seventh Crusade (and persecuted Cathars). The **Tour de Constance** (www.tourdeconstance.com; adult/child €8/free; ⊙10am-7pm May-Aug, to 5.30pm Sep-Apr; 👤) once held Huguenot prisoners; today it's the start of the 1.6km wall-top circuit, a must-do for heady views of salt mountains and viridian plains. Park on bd Diderot, on the outside of the northwestern wall.

Plage de Piémanson

⑥ Domaine de la Palissade (p72)

Along the D36D, **Domaine de la Palissade** (📞04 42 86 81 28; www.palissade.fr; 36 chemin Départemental; adult/child €3/free; 🕐9am-6pm mid-Jun–mid-Sep, to 5pm Mar–mid-Jun & mid-Sep–Oct, 9am-5pm Wed-Sun Feb & Nov; 🅿️) organises horse treks (€19 per hour) where you'll find yourself wading across brackish lakes and through a purple haze of sea lavender. It will also take you around lagoons and scrubby glasswort on foot, or give you a free map of the estate's marked walking trails. Don't forget to rent binoculars; best €2 you'll spend this trip!

The Drive » The next 3.7km along the rte de la Mer is equally enchanting, with flocks of birds circling and salt crystals flashing in the sun. Stop at the sea.

TRIP HIGHLIGHT

⑦ Plage de Piémanson

Just try to resist the urge to greet the Med with a wild dash into the waves at this lovely, windswept beach. Unusually, camping is allowed here from May to September, and hundreds of campervans line up along the dunes for the duration of the *belle saison*. It's a scene that's as polarising of opinion as it is spectacular. Basic facilities and a patrolled section of sand are right at the end of rte de la Mer; head east for the popular nudist beach.

The Drive » Backtrack north along the D36. Just before Salin de Giraud, look for a car park and a small black shack on your right.

⑧ Le Point de Vue

This lookout provides a rare vantage point to take in the stunning scene of pink-stained *salins* (salt pans) and soaring crystalline mountains. As

BIRDLIFE OF THE CAMARGUE

The largest wetland in France, home (at least part of the year) to around two-thirds of Europe's bird species, the Camargue is an ornithological wonderland. A national park since 1970, it's a vital waypoint on migratory routes between Europe and Africa.

Within the 930 sq km national park, coexisting with farms producing Camarguais rice, bulls and horses, lies a Unesco-protected biosphere of 131 sq km, in which more than 300 bird species have been observed.

Amongst the best sites for birdwatchers include Marais du Vigueirat, Domaine de la Palissade (p47), Pont de Gau (p45) and La Capelière (p46).

Vigueirat offers 15km of trails through 11.2 sq km of marshland, with purple herons and great spotted cuckoos present in summer, booted eagles in winter, spoonbills and terns during migratory periods, and bitterns and egrets year-round.

Palissade has varying trails from 1km to 8km through a section that hasn't been tamed by artificial embankments. You can see spectacled warblers in summer, greylag geese in winter, migrating curlews, and mallards year-round.

Pont de Gau is a 60-hectare sanctuary and veterinary centre with 7km of trails affording sightings of hoopoes in summer, marsh harriers in winter, migrating storks, and grey- and night-heron year-round.

La Capelière, at 13 sq km, is the largest single reserve in the park, with a visitor centre open year-round. There's the chance to spot redshanks and reed warblers in summer, snipe and tufted ducks in winter, migratory plovers and kingfishers throughout the year.

---

fruitful as it is beguiling, this is Europe's largest salt works, producing some 800,000 tonnes per year. A small shop (the aforementioned black shack) sells *sel de Camargue* (Camargue salt) by the pot or sack, bull-meat sausages and tins of fragrant local olive oil.

The Drive » Heading north on D36 for 20 minutes, Le Mas de Peint is on your right before Le Sambuc, while La Chassagnette's fork and trowel shingle is on the left to its north.

---

9 Le Sambuc

This sleepy town's outskirts hide away one of the region's most luxurious places to stay, and one of its best restaurants. **Le Mas de Peint** (☎04 90 97 20 62; www.masdepeint. com; rte de Salin de Giraud, Le Sambuc, Manade Jacques Bon; d €250; ⊙mid-Mar–mid-Nov; ❋ ☎ ☎) is owned by the Le Bon family, who have been in the *gardian* (cowboy) business for decades. Along with superb food and lovely rooms, the hotel also offers flamenco, bull-herding and bird-watching weekends.

The Drive » Continue north on the D36, where you'll re-meet the D570 heading to Arles.

---

10 Arles (p65)

Back in Arles, last stop is **Les Arènes** (Amphithéâtre; ☎08 91 70 03 70; www. arenes-arles.com; Rond-Point des Arènes; adult/child €6/free, incl Théâtre Antique €9/free; ⊙9am-8pm Jul & Aug, to 7pm May, Jun & Sep, shorter hours Oct-Apr), the town's incredibly well-preserved Roman amphitheatre. Dating from around AD 90, this great arena would once have held more than 21,000 blood-thirsty spectators, and it's still used for many events. The structure itself hasn't survived the centuries entirely intact, but it's still an evocative insight into the Roman psyche. Entry is on the northern side.

Heron, Parc Ornithologique de Pont du Gau (p45)

Destinations

Nîmes & Around (p52)
A magnificient Roman amphitheatre, museums and markets compete for attention in this bustling commercial area.

Provence (p59)
With its picturesque lavender fields and delectable cuisine, Provence is a feast for the senses.

French Riviera (p89)
Life's a beach in this idyllic region, as popular for its sun, sea and sand as it is for its arts scene.

Promenade des Anglais (p91), Nice
VALERY BARETA/SHUTTERSTOCK ©

Nîmes is a busy commercial city these days, but two millennia ago it was one of the most important cities of Roman Gaul.

Nîmes & Around

NÎMES

Links to Nîmes' past are clearly illustrated by the city's collection of Roman buildings, including a magnificent amphitheatre and a 2000-year-old temple.

There are plenty of museums and markets to explore in Nîmes' palm-lined streets, as well as a host of high-profile festivals throughout the year. Nîmes is also proud of the futuristic Musée de la Romanité, which opened in mid-2018 and is one of the best archaeological museums in Languedoc-Roussillon. In 2018, Nîmes applied – to no avail – to be listed as a Unesco World Heritage Site.

⊙ Sights

★ Les Arènes   ROMAN SITES
(☑ 04 66 21 82 56; www.arenes-nimes.com; place des Arènes; adult/child incl audioguide €10/8; ☉ 9am-8pm Jul & Aug, to 6.30pm Apr-Jun & Sep, to 6pm Mar & Oct, 9.30am-5pm Jan, Feb, Nov & Dec) Nîmes' twin-tiered amphitheatre is the best preserved in France. Built around 100 BC, the arena once seated 24,000 spectators and staged gladiatorial contests and public executions; it's still an impressive venue for gigs and events. An audioguide provides context as you explore the arena, seating areas, stairwells and

corridors (known to Romans as *vomitories*), and afterwards you can view replicas of gladiatorial armour and original bullfighters' costumes in the museum.

At 133m long, 101m wide and 21m high, with an oval arena encircled by two tiers of arches and columns, the amphitheatre is a testament to the skill and ingenuity of Roman architects. Despite being adapted, plundered for stone and generally abused over many centuries, the structure of the amphitheatre is still largely intact, and it's not hard to imagine what the atmosphere must have been like when it was filled to capacity.

The seating is divided into four tiers and 34 rows; the posher you were, the closer you sat to the centre. The amphitheatre's oval design meant everyone had an unrestricted view. A system of trapdoors and hoist-lifts beneath the arena enabled animals and combatants to be put into position during the show. Originally, the amphitheatre would have had a canopy that protected spectators from the weather.

Musée de la Romanité   MUSEUM
(☑ 04 48 21 02 10; 16 bd des Arènes; adult/child €8/3; ☉ 10am-8pm Jul & Aug, to 7pm Sep-Nov & Apr-Jun, to 6pm Wed-Mon Dec-Mar) Opened in mid-2018, this futuristic steel-and-glass structure faces Les Arènes right in the heart of the city.

Maison Carrée

Within, the ambitious archaeological museum's permanent exhibitions are devoted to regional archaeology, with more than 5000 artefacts including well-preserved mosaics and ceramics.

Maison Carrée
ROMAN SITE

(☑ 04 66 21 82 56; www.maisoncarree.eu; place de la Maison Carrée; adult/child €6/5; ☺ 9.30am-8pm Jul & Aug, 10am-6.30pm Apr-Jun & Sep, to 6pm Mar & Oct, to 1pm & 2-4.30pm Jan, Feb, Nov & Dec) Constructed in gleaming limestone around AD 5, this temple was built to honour Emperor Augustus' two adopted sons. Despite the name, the Maison Carrée (Square House) is actually rectangular – to the Romans, 'square' simply meant a building with right angles. The building is beautifully preserved, complete with stately columns and triumphal steps. There's no need to go inside unless you're interested in the relatively cheesy 22-minute 3D film.

Jardins de la Fontaine
PARK

(quai de la Fontaine; adult/child €3.50/3, garden free; ☺ 9am-8pm Jul & Aug, to 5pm Sep-Jun) Roman remains in these elegant gardens include the 30m-high Tour Magne, raised around 15 BC – the largest of a chain of towers conveying imperial power that once punctuated the city's 7km-long Roman ramparts. At the top of its 140 steps, an orientation table interprets the panoramic views over Nîmes.

The gardens also shelter the Source de la Fontaine – once the site of a spring, temple and baths – and the crumbling Temple de Diane, located in the northwest corner.

Carré d'Art – Musée d'Art Contemporain
GALLERY

(☑ 04 66 76 35 70; www.carreartmusee.com; 16 place de la Maison Carrée; ☺ 10am-6pm Tue-Sun) FREE The striking glass-and-steel Carré d'Art was designed by British architect Sir Norman Foster. Inside is the Musée d'Art Contemporain, with permanent and temporary exhibitions covering art from the 1960s onwards. The rooftop restaurant (open Wednesday to Sunday) makes a lovely spot for a drink.

Musée du Vieux Nîmes
MUSEUM

(☑ 04 66 76 73 70; place aux Herbes; adult/child €5/free; ☺ 10am-6pm Tue-Sun) Inside the city's 17th-century episcopal palace, the town museum delves into the history of Nîmes from

INFO:
PASS NÎMES ROMAINE

Save money by purchasing a Pass Nîmes Romaine (Roman Nîmes Pass) combination ticket (adult/child €13/11), which covers admission to Les Arènes, Maison Carrée and Tour Magne at Jardins de la Fontaine. The pass is valid for three days and can be bought at any of these three sites.

Nîmes

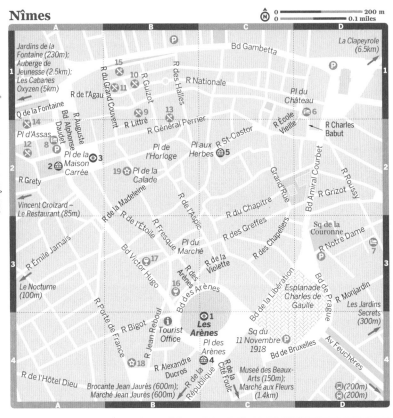

Nîmes

Roman times through to the modern era, with lots of period costumes and a display of denim-wearing celebrities including Elvis and Marilyn Monroe.

🎊 Festivals & Events

Les Grands Jeux Romains   CULTURAL
(www.arenes-nimes.com; ⏰late Apr) For three days in April, Romans reconquer the town

with an encampment, staged gladiatorial battles in Les Arènes and a triumphal street parade.

Jeudis de Nîmes   CULTURAL

(⊙Jul & Aug) Between 6pm and 10.30pm every Thursday in July and August, food markets and live gigs take over Nîmes' squares.

🛏 Sleeping

Auberge de Jeunesse   HOSTEL €

(🖉04 66 68 03 20; www.hifrance.org/auberge-de-jeunesse/nimes.html; 257 chemin de l'Auberge de Jeunesse, La Cigale; camping per person €9, dm/d incl breakfast €24/50; ⊙reception 7.30am-11pm, hostel closed Nov-Feb; 🅿🛜) It's out in the sticks, 4km northwest of the bus and train stations, but this well-managed hostel has lots in its favour: spacious four- to eight-bed dorms (some with their own bathroom), double rooms, a large garden, a self-catering kitchen, a laundry and a cafe. Take bus 9, direction Alès or Villeverte, and get off at the Stade stop.

Hôtel des Tuileries   HOTEL €

(🖉04 66 21 31 15; www.hoteldestuileries.com; 22 rue Roussy; d €60-93, tr €70-93, ste €85-118; 🅿✳🛜) This well-priced 11-room hotel within strolling distance from Les Arènes features simple yet satisfyingly equipped rooms, some with covered balconies. Breakfast costs €9. Its private parking garage (€10 to €15) is just down the street, but there are only five car spaces, so reserve ahead.

Hôtel Central   HOTEL €

(🖉04 66 67 27 75; www.hotel-central.org; 2 place du Château; d €60-95; ✳🛜) Rooms at this aptly named hotel in Nîmes' heart have wooden floors, neutral colours and sleek bathrooms. *Supérieure* rooms offer the most space. Rooms on the top floor have great city views, but the lack of a lift is a drawback considering the number of stairs.

Royal Hôtel   HOTEL €€

(🖉04 66 58 28 27; www.royalhotel-nimes.com; 3 bd Alphonse Daudet; d €80-125; ✳🛜) Bedrooms here have modern-meets-heritage decor and a choice of street views or an outlook over the grand place d'Assas – fine for the view, though the noise might be intrusive on summer nights. They're split into standard and superior; it's worth bumping up a level for extra space. A few rooms have renovated bathrooms. No lift, alas.

🍴 Eating

A tempting array of restaurants and cafeterias is dotted around the centre. Place aux Herbes, place de l'Horloge and place du Marché are great places to watch the world drift languidly by at bistros, cafes and bars with pavement seating.

La Petite Fadette   TEAHOUSE €

(🖉04 66 67 53 05; 34 rue du Grand Couvent; menus €15-24, mains €10-20; ⊙11am-2.30pm Mon-Wed, 11am-2.30pm & 6-10pm Thu-Sat) *Tartines* (open-face toasted sandwiches) such as ham and tomato or fig jam and goat's cheese, as well as huge salads, are specialities of this cosy *salon de thé* (tearoom), which has a cute rococo interior and outside tables on a small courtyard. A platter of tapas (€20) is also available. Wash it down with a glass of organic wine.

La Marmite   BISTRO €

(🖉04 66 29 98 23; www.facebook.com/impeccable.30; 6 rue de l'Agau; menus €13-25; ⊙noon-2pm Mon-Sat & 7.30-9.30pm Thu-Sat) The *menu* changes almost daily depending on what the chef considers the best local produce at the nearby Halles, and specials – always flavoursome – are scribbled on the well-worn blackboard. It's always packed with local connoisseurs who won't consider eating anywhere else, so book ahead.

L'Imprévu   FRENCH €

(🖉04 66 38 99 59; www.l-imprevu.com; 6 place d'Assas; menus €19-24, mains €13-24; ⊙noon-2pm & 7.30-10.30pm Thu-Tue) Tucked away in the corner of place d'Assas, this fine-dining bistro has a sheltered interior courtyard and a terrace. There's a good choice of seafood, meats and pastas, and some superb desserts such as Breton shortbread with caramelised pears and green-apple sorbet.

Aux Plaisirs des Halles   FRENCH €€

(🖉04 66 36 01 02; www.auxplaisirsdeshalles.com; 4 rue Littré; menus €25-44, mains €23-26; ⊙noon-2pm & 7.30-10pm Tue-Sat) Market-fresh dining – veal, beef, chicken, fresh fish – is the order of the day here, served with an excellent choice of Languedoc wines. The mains are quite expensive, so consider swinging by for the good-value lunch *menu*. It's just along from the covered market. Eat in the cosy interior or quiet, shaded rear courtyard.

Le Nocturne   BISTRO €€

(🖉04 66 67 20 28; www.restaurant-le-nocturne. com; 29bis rue Benoît Malon; menus €25-50, mains €21-28; ⊙8pm-1am Wed-Sun; 🖉) Late-opening

TOP TIP:
CANOEING ON THE RIVER GARD

For a unique perspective on the Pont du Gard, you need to see it from the water. The Gard River flows from the Cévennes mountains all the way to the aqueduct, passing through the dramatic Gorges du Gardon en route. The best time to do it is between April and June, as winter floods and summer droughts can sometimes make the river impassable.

Most of the local hire companies are based in Collias, 8km from the bridge, a journey of about two hours by kayak. Depending on the season and the height of the river, you can make a longer journey by being dropped upstream at Pont St-Nicholas (19km, about five hours) or Russan (32km, seven to eight hours); the latter option also includes a memorable trip through the Gorges du Gardon.

There's a minimum age of six. Life jackets are always provided, but you must be a competent swimmer. Operators include the following:

Canoë Collias (☑ 04 66 22 87 20; www.canoe-collias.com; 194 chemin de St-Privat, Collias; adult/child €23/12; ⊗ 8am-8pm mid-Mar–late Oct)

Canoë Le Tourbillon (p21)

Kayak Vert (p21)

Le Nocturne is a fine place to dine on rich southwestern flavours. Duck and beef dominate the menu, but there are also appetising fish and veggie options. Rare vintages and limited releases from small-scale producers make up the wine list. There are just 26 seats, so book ahead.

Le Carré d'Art　　　　　　　　FRENCH €€
(☑ 04 66 67 52 40; www.restaurant-lecarredart.com; 2 rue Gaston Boissier; menus €17-29, mains €23-26; ⊗ noon-1.45pm & 8-10pm Tue-Sat) Open since 1989, this long-standing institution is still going strong. The setting is elegant, in an abstract-art-adorned 19th-century townhouse with a gorgeous shaded courtyard, and the seasonal dishes give traditional French cuisine a modern spin.

**Vincent Croizard –
Le Restaurant**　　　　　　GASTRONOMY €€€
(☑ 04 66 67 04 99; www.restaurantcroizard.com; 17 rue des Chassaintes; menus €23-58, mains €18-42; ⊗ 12.15-1.30pm & 7.45-9.15pm Wed-Sun) From its discreet façade on a quiet side street, you'd never guess that this restaurant is home to an impossibly romantic lamplit courtyard garden and some of Nîmes' most inventive and artistic high-end cooking. Dishes use premium produce from Languedoc (fresh fish, pork, veal and oysters, among others). Pick from its long and choice selection of French wines.

Les Halles　　　　　　　　　　　MARKET €
(www.leshallesdenimes.com; rues Guizot, Général Perrier & des Halles; ⊗ 7am-1pm Mon-Sat, to 1.30pm Sun) With over 100 stalls in 3500 sq metres, Nîmes' covered market is the best place for supplies. Look out for local specialities including *picholines* – a local green olive with its own AOP (Appellation d'Origine Protégée) – and *brandade* (salt cod). You'll also find a couple of great eateries.

🍷 Drinking & Nightlife

La Grande Bourse　　　　　　　　　BAR
(2 bd des Arènes; ⊗ 8am-midnight) A spectacular location and a large terrace directly opposite Les Arènes (p52) means this opulent 19th-century cafe gleaming with chandeliers and mirrors gets packed with tourists in high season, when service can move at a snail's pace. Avoid the food.

Mercadante　　　　　　　　　　SICILIAN €
(☑ 04 66 23 01 41; http://mercadante.free.fr; 4 bd Gambetta; menus €16-21, mains €10-22; ⊗ 11.45am-2pm & 7.45-10pm Tue-Sat) Sicilian brothers Fabio and Salvo Mercadante serve the classic flavours of their homeland at their little den overlooking a busy thoroughfare. Expect tasty spaghetti, penne, lasagne, cured meat, fish and meat dishes as well as a small yet tempting selection of *dolci* (desserts). Service is slow.

Le Café Olive BAR
(📞 04 66 67 89 10; 22 bd Victor Hugo; ⏰ 9am-11pm Mon-Fri, 6-11pm Sat & Sun) Stone walls and dim lighting give this little nightspot a cosy, cavern-like ambience. There are regular gigs and a great choice of wines by the glass. It also serves food.

Entertainment

Les Arènes is the major venue for outdoor spectacles such as concerts, pageants and bullfights.

Ciné Sémaphore CINEMA
(📞 04 66 67 83 11; www.cinema-semaphore.fr; 25 rue Porte de France; tickets adult/child €7/5.50) Five screens showing *version originale* (VO, or undubbed) films.

Théâtre de Nîmes PERFORMING ARTS
(📞 04 66 36 02 04; http://theatredenimes.com; 1 place de la Calade) Renowned venue for drama and music.

Shopping

Regular markets are held in Nîmes through-out the week.

Brocante Jean Jaurès MARKET
(av Jean Jaurès; ⏰ 8am-1pm Mon) Nîmes' weekly flea market sells bric-a-brac and antiques.

Marché Jean Jaurès MARKET
(bd Jean Jaurès; ⏰ 7am-1pm Fri) Local produce fills Nîmes' weekly farmers market.

Marché aux Fleurs MARKET
(av de la Bouvine; ⏰ 7am-6pm Mon) Flower mar-ket held outside the Stade des Costières foot-ball stadium.

ⓘ Information

Tourist Office (📞 04 66 58 38 00; www.nimes-tourisme.com; 6 bd des Arènes; ⏰ 9am-7.30pm Mon-Fri, to 7pm Sat, 10am-6pm Sun Jul & Aug, 9am-6pm Mon-Fri, to 5pm Sat, 10am-5pm Sun Sep-Jun; 📶) Plenty of info on Nîmes and the surrounding region.

ⓘ Getting There & Around

AIR

Aéroport de Nîmes Alès Camargue Cévennes (FNI; 📞 04 66 70 49 49; www.aeroport-nimes. fr; St-Gilles) Nîmes' airport, 10km southeast of the city on the A54, is served only by Ryanair, which flies to/from London Luton, Liverpool, Brussels-Charleroi and Fez.

An airport bus (€6.80, 30 minutes) to/from the **train station** (bd Sergent Triaire) connects with all flights.

CAR & MOTORCYCLE

Major car-rental companies have kiosks at the airport and the train station.

AROUND NÎMES

Sights & Activities

⭐Pont du Gard ROMAN SITE
(📞 04 66 37 50 99; www.pontdugard.fr; adult/child €8.50/6, Pass Aqueduc incl guided visit of topmost tier €11.50/6; ⏰ 9am-11pm Jul & Aug, to 10pm Jun & Sep, to 9pm May, to 8pm Apr & Oct, to 6pm Nov-Mar) The extraordinary three-tiered Pont du Gard was once part of a 50km-long system of channels built around 19 BC to transport water from Uzès to Nîmes. The scale is huge: the bridge is 48.8m high, 275m long and graced with 52 precision-built arches. It was the highest in the Roman Empire. At the visitors centre on the left, northern bank, there's an im-pressive, high-tech museum featuring the bridge, the aqueduct and the role of water in Roman society.

Each block was carved by hand and trans-ported from nearby quarries – no mean feat, considering the largest blocks weighed over 5 tonnes. The height of the bridge descends by 2.5cm across its length, providing just enough gradient to keep the water flowing – an amazing demonstration of the precision of Roman engineering.

You can walk across the tiers for pan-oramic views over the Gard River, but the best perspective on the bridge is from downstream, along the 1.4km Mémoires de Garrigue walking trail. If you buy the Pass Aqueduc, you can walk the bridge's topmost tier, along which the water flowed (guided tour). For children, there's Ludo, an activity play area.

Early evening is a good time to visit, as admission is cheaper (adult/child €5/3) and the bridge is stunningly illuminated after dark.

It's 21km northeast of Nîmes.

There are large car parks on both banks of the river that are a 400m level walk from the Pont du Gard.

Several buses stop in Collias and Remou-lins (near Pont du Gard), including Edgard bus B21 (€1.50, two or three daily Monday to Saturday, one or two on Sunday) between Nîmes and Uzès.

Musée Perrier
MUSEUM

(📞 04 66 87 61 01; www.perrier.com; Les Bouillens, Vergèze; adult/child €3/2, tours €5/3; ⊘9.30am-12.30pm & 1.30-5pm Mon-Fri Apr-Sep) World-famous fizzy water Perrier has its source in natural springs 13km southwest of Nîmes. You can watch a 3D film that explains Perrier's history, the production process and the reason behind the bottle's iconic shape (spoiler: it's to do with pressure), and pick up Perrier-themed souvenirs in the shop. Guided tours take you to the springs.

The main plant supplies around 900 million bottles every year.

Uzès

Storybook-pretty Uzès is renowned for its Renaissance architecture, a reminder of the days when it was an important trading centre – especially for silk, linen and liquorice. But it also has strong Roman links: water was delivered here via the Pont du Gard aqueduct (p57) en route to Nîmes, 25km to the southwest.

Highlights here include the ducal palace, the cathedral (place de l'Évêché; ⊘9am-6pm May-Sep, to 5pm Oct-Apr), elegant mansions and the arcaded central square, place aux Herbes, which hosts a lively farmers market every Wednesday and Saturday. For foodies, Uzès' biggest appeal is its cache of sublime places to dine.

- - - - - - - - - - - - - - - - - - - -

⊙ Sights

★ Duché
CHATEAU

(📞 04 66 22 18 96; www.uzes.fr; place du Duché; €13, incl tour €18; ⊘10am-12.30pm & 2-6.30pm Jul & Aug, to noon & 2-6pm Sep-Jun) This fortified château belonged to the House of Crussol, who were the dukes of Uzès for over 1000 years until the French Revolution. The building is a Renaissance wonder, with a majestic 16th-century façade showing the three orders of classical architecture (Ionic, Doric and Corinthian). Inside, guided tours (in French) take in the lavish ducal apartments and 800-year-old cellars; you can climb the 135-step Bermonde tower for wrap-around town views.

Jardin Médiéval
GARDENS

(Medieval Garden; http://jardinmedievaluzes.com; rue Port Royal; adult/child garden & Tour du Roi €5.50/3; ⊘10.30am-12.30pm & 2-6pm Jul & Aug, 2-6pm Mon-Fri, 10.30am-12.30pm & 2-6pm Sat & Sun Apr-Jun, Sep & Oct, closed Nov-Mar) This delightful garden contains a wealth of plants and flowers that served a variety of purposes for their medieval planters: medicinal, nutritional and symbolic. Climbing 100 steps inside the Tour du Roi (King's Tower) rewards with panoramic views over Uzès' rooftops.

Musée du Bonbon Haribo
MUSEUM

(Sweets Museum; 📞 04 66 22 20 25; www.museeharibo.fr; Pont des Charrettes; adult/child €7.50/5.50; ⊘9.30am-7pm Jul & Aug, 10am-1pm & 2-6pm Tue-Sun Sep-Jun) Uzès' history as a confectionery centre lives on at this Wonka-esque museum, which explores the sweets-making process from the early 20th century through to the present day. There's a collection of antique advertising posters and vintage confectionery machinery, but inevitably it's the rainbow-coloured sweets shop that takes centre stage. It's 4km southeast of town.

ⓘ Information

Tourist Office (📞 04 66 22 68 88; www.pays-uzes-tourisme.com; place Albert 1er; ⊘10am-6pm Mon-Fri, 10am-1pm & 2-5pm Sat & Sun Jun-Sep, 10am-12.30pm & 2-6pm Mon-Fri, 10am-1pm Sat Oct-May) Just outside the old quarter. Has free leaflets (in English and French) describing walking tours of the historical centre.

ⓘ Getting There & Away

Local **buses** (av de la Gare) are run by Edgard (www.edgard-transport.fr).

Alès Line A15, €1.50, one hour, five to six daily Monday to Friday, three on weekends

Avignon Line A15, €1.50, one hour, five daily Monday to Friday, three on weekends

Nîmes Line E52, €1.50, one hour, eight to 10 daily Monday to Friday, three or four on weekends

Provence

Provence evokes picture-postcard images of lavender fields, medieval hilltop villages, bustling markets and superb food and wine.

While the Vaucluse and Luberon epitomise the Provençal cliché, if you go a little deeper, you'll find Provence's incredible diversity. Near the mouth of the Rhône in the Camargue, craggy limestone yields to bleached salt marshes specked pink with flamingos, and the light, which so captivated Van Gogh and Cézanne, begins to change. Then there's the serpentine Gorges du Verdon, its pea-green water lorded over by half-mile-high limestone walls and craggy mountain peaks beyond. The region's other *belle surprises* are its cities: bohemian Aix and Roman Arles.

Constant across the region is the food – clean, bright flavours, as simple as sweet tomatoes drizzled with olive oil and sprinkled with *fleur de sel* (sea salt) from the Camargue.

History

Settled over the centuries by the Ligurians, the Celts and the Greeks, the area between the Alps, the sea and the Rhône River flourished following Julius Caesar's conquest in the mid-1st century BC. The Romans called the area Provincia Romana, which evolved into the name Provence. After the collapse of the Roman Empire in the late 5th century Provence was invaded several times, by the Visigoths, Burgundians and Ostrogoths.

During the 14th century, the Catholic Church, under a series of French-born popes, moved its headquarters from feud-riven Rome to Avignon, thus beginning the most resplendent period in the city's (and region's) history. Provence became part of France in 1481, but Avignon and Carpentras remained under papal control until the Revolution.

Aix-en-Provence

POP 142,668

A pocket of left-bank Parisian chic deep in Provence, Aix (pronounced like the letter X) is all class: its leafy boulevards and public squares are lined with 17th- and 18th-century mansions, punctuated by gurgling moss-covered fountains. Haughty stone lions guard its grandest avenue, cafe-laced cours Mirabeau, where fashionable Aixois pose on polished pavement terraces, sipping espresso. While Aix is a student hub, its upmarket appeal makes it pricier than other Provençal towns.

The part-pedestrianised centre of Aix' old town is ringed by busy boulevards, with several large car parks dotted on the edge of town. Whatever you do, don't try and drive into the centre.

Aix-en-Provence

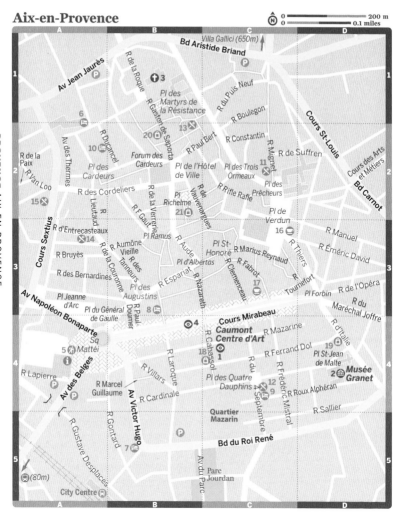

⊙ Sights

A stroller's paradise, the highlight is the mostly pedestrian old city, Vieil Aix. South of cours Mirabeau, the Quartier Mazarin was laid out in the 17th century, and is home to some of Aix' finest buildings and a square: place des Quatre Dauphins, with its fish-spouting fountain (1667), is enchanting.

Cours Mirabeau   CYCLING

No streetscape better epitomises Provence's most graceful city than this 440m-long, fountain-studded street, sprinkled with Renaissance *hôtels particuliers* (private man-

sions) and crowned with a summertime roof of leafy plane trees. It was laid out in the 1650s and later named after the Revolutionary hero the Comte de Mirabeau. Cézanne and Zola hung out at Les Deux Garçons (☑ 04 42 26 00 51; http://lesdeuxgarcons.fr; 53 cours Mirabeau; ⊙7am-2am), one of a string of busy pavement cafes.

★Musée Granet   MUSEUM

(☑04 42 52 88 32; www.museegranet-aixen provence.fr; place St-Jean de Malte; adult/child €5.50/free; ⊙10am-7pm Tue-Sun mid-Jun–Sep, noon-6pm Tue-Sun Oct–mid-Jun) Aix established

Aix-en-Provence

one of France's first public museums here, on the site of a former Hospitallers' priory, in 1838. Nearly 200 years of acquisitions (including bequests by the eponymous François Marius Granet, himself a painter of note) have resulted in a collection of more than 12,000 works, including pieces by Picasso, Léger, Matisse, Monet, Klee, Van Gogh and, crucially, nine pieces by local boy Cézanne. This fabulous art museum sits right near the top of France's artistic must-sees.

★ **Caumont Centre d'Art**   HISTORIC BUILDING
(☑04 42 20 70 01; www.caumont-centredart.com; 3 rue Joseph Cabassol; adult/child €6.50/free; ⊙10am-7pm May-Sep, to 6pm Oct-Apr) The Caumont is a stellar art space housed inside the Mazarin quarter's grandest 18th-century *hôtel particulier*. While there are three quality exhibitions each year, plus concerts and other events, it's the building itself that's the star of the show. Built from local honey-coloured stone, its palatial rooms are stuffed with antiques and objets d'art attesting to the opulence of the house's aristocratic past.

Cathédrale St-Sauveur   CATHEDRAL
(34 place des Martyrs-de-la-Résistance; ⊙cathedral 8am-7.30pm, cloisters 10am-noon & 2-5.30pm) Built between 1285 and 1350 in a potpourri of styles, this cathedral includes a Romanesque 12th-century nave in its southern aisle, chapels from the 14th and 15th centuries, and a 5th-century sarcophagus in the apse. More recent additions include the 18th-century gilt Baroque organ. Acoustics make Sunday-afternoon Gregorian chants

unforgettable. The entire ensemble sits over the vanished 1st-century Roman forum.

Fondation Victor Vasarely   GALLERY
(☑04 42 20 01 09; www.fondationvasarely.org; 1 av Marcel Pagnol; adult/child €9/4; ⊙10am-6pm; ⓟ) This gallery, 4km west of the city, was designed by Hungarian optical-art innovator Victor Vasarely (1906–97). An architectural masterpiece, it has 16 interconnecting, hexagonal galleries purpose-built to display and reflect the patterning of the artist's 44 acid-trip-ready, floor-to-ceiling geometric artworks. Take bus 2 to the Vasarely stop.

✵ Festivals & Events

★ **Festival d'Aix-en-Provence**   MUSIC
(☑04 34 08 02 17; www.festival-aix.com; ⊙Jul) Established in the spirit of rebirth following WWII, this world-renowned festival brings opera, orchestral works, chamber music and even buskers to Aix throughout July. The wonderfully atmospheric Théâtre de l'Archevêché, created for the first festival in 1948 and still its principal venue, occupies the courtyard of the former Archbishop's Palace.

⊨ Sleeping

★ **L'Épicerie**   B&B €€
(☑06 74 40 89 73; 12 rue du Cancel; r from €110; ☎) It's best to connect by phone to this intimate B&B on a backstreet in Vieil Aix. The creation of born-and-bred Aixois lad Luc, the breakfast room re-creates a 1950s grocery

store, while the flowery garden out the back is perfect for evening dining and weekend brunch (book ahead for both). Breakfast is a veritable feast. Two rooms accommodate families of four.

★ Hôtel les Quatre Dauphins
BOUTIQUE HOTEL €€

(📞04 42 38 16 39; www.lesquatredauphins.fr; 54 rue Roux Alphéran; s/d €101/123; ❄🖹) This sweet 13-room hotel slumbers in a former 19th-century mansion in one of the loveliest parts of town. Rooms are fresh and clean, decorated with a great eye and equipped with excellent modern bathrooms. Those with sloping, beamed ceilings in the attic are quaint but are not for those who don't pack light – the terracotta-tiled staircase is not suitcase friendly.

Hôtel des Augustins
HOTEL €€

(📞04 42 27 28 59; www.hotel-augustins.com; 3 rue de la Masse; s/d €139/159; ❄🖹) Once a 15th-century Augustinian convent – the magnificent stone-vaulted lobby makes visible use of an earlier, 12th-century chapel – this charismatic hotel has volumes of history. Martin Luther even stayed here after his excommunication. Sadly, there's not so much heritage to be found in the modern rooms, though pricier suites have antique furniture and private terraces beneath the bell tower.

Hôtel Aquabella
HOTEL €€

(📞04 42 99 15 00; www.aquabella.fr; 2 rue des Étuves; r from €143; ❄🖹🏊) Attached to Aix's thermal spa, this four-star hotel knows how to pamper: rates include access to the Sensory spa, with a Finnish sauna, two *hammams* (Turkish baths), a pool and a fitness centre. The modern building itself has more corporate charm than charisma, but the rooms are contemporary and very comfortable. Check out online packages for best value.

★ Villa Gallici
HISTORIC HOTEL €€€

(📞04 42 23 29 23; www.villagallici.com; 18 av de la Violette; r from €560; 🅿❄🖹🏊) Baroque and beautiful, this fabulous villa was built as a private residence in the 18th century and still feels marvellously opulent. Rooms are more like museum pieces, stuffed with gilded mirrors, *toile de Jouy* wallpaper and filigreed furniture. There's a lovely lavender-filled garden to breakfast in, plus a pool, a superb restaurant and a wine cellar.

Hôtel Cézanne
BOUTIQUE HOTEL €€€

(📞04 42 91 11 11; www.hotelaix.com; 40 av Victor Hugo; d/ste €310/410; 🅿❄@🖹) This striking design hotel acknowledges Aix' painterly pedigree with a life-sized Cézanne figure, abstract sculptures and huge panels of modern art. The rooms perhaps don't justify the price (to which €20 per person is added for an admittedly outstanding breakfast), but

DON'T MISS:
CÉZANNE SIGHTS

The life of local lad Paul Cézanne (1839–1906) is treasured in Aix. To see where he ate, drank, studied and painted, follow the Circuit de Cézanne (Cézanne Trail), marked by footpath-embedded bronze plaques. Pick up the accompanying information booklet at the tourist office.

Cézanne's last studio, Atelier Cézanne (p40), 1.5km north of the tourist office on a hilltop, was painstakingly preserved (and recreated: not all the tools and still-life models strewn around the single room were his) as it was at the time of his death. Though the studio is inspiring, none of his works hang here. Films are screened in the garden in July and August. Further uphill is the Terrain des Peintres (p41), a terraced garden perfect for a picnic, from where Cézanne painted the Montagne Ste-Victoire.

Visits to the other two sights must be reserved in advance at the tourist office. In 1859 Cézanne's father bought Bastide du Jas de Bouffan (p41), a country manor west of Aix, where Cézanne painted furiously: 36 oils and 17 watercolours in the decades that followed depicting the house, farm and chestnut-lined alley. It's a 20-minute walk from town.

In 1895 Cézanne rented a cabin at Les Carrières de Bibémus (p41), on the edge of town, where he painted prolifically and where he did most of his Montagne Ste-Victoire paintings. Atmospheric one-hour tours of the ochre quarry take visitors on foot through the dramatic burnt-orange rocks Cézanne captured so vividly.

Cours Mirabeau (p60)

fancy extras like iMacs, a brace of hip bars, free Nespresso refills and free parking tip the balance.

✕ Eating

Aix excels at Provençal cuisine. Restaurant terraces spill out across dozens of charm-heavy old-town squares, many pierced by ancient stone fountains; place des Trois Ormeaux, place des Augustins, place Ramus and vast Forum des Cardeurs are particular favourites.

★ Farinoman Fou   BAKERY €
(www.farinomanfou.fr; 3 rue Mignet; bread €1.40-3; ⊙7am-7pm Tue-Sat) To appeal to bread con-noisseurs, in Aix as in any part of France, you need to know your dough. Judging by the lines typically spilling out of this shop onto place des Prêcheurs, artisanal *bou-langer* Benoît Fradette clearly does. The bakery has no need to invest in a fancy shop-front – customers jostle for space with bread ovens and dough-mixing tubs.

Maison Nosh   CAFE €
(⌇06 52 86 22 39; www.maison-nosh.com; 42-44 cours Sextius; lunch menus €10-12; ⊙10am-6pm Mon-Sat) Branching out from its original menu of posh hot dogs and gourmet Eng-lish muffins, this breezy, youthful cafe now offers healthier breakfast, brunch and lunch options, and it's a pleasant place to linger over excellent coffee. Gourmet hot dogs and muffins still form the core of the lunchtime *formules,* however: for €10 you also get a dessert and a drink.

Le Bistrot   BISTRO €
(⌇04 42 23 34 61; 5 Rue Campra; plat du jour €10, lunch menu €16, mains €15-16; ⊙noon-2pm & 7.30-10pm) Locals pack into the tiny vaulted din-ing room of this hard-to-find place for the superb-value lunch *menus.* All the bistro boxes are ticked: red-and-white tablecloths, friendly old-school service, a chuffing cof-fee machine and menu classics like *daube provençal* (meat stew), chicken hotpot and grilled entrecôte. Extra points for the witty names: the chocolate mousse is called 'Look out, moustache-wearers'.

CALISSONS D'AIX

Aix' sweetest treat since King René's wedding banquet in 1473 is the marzipan-like local speciality, *calis-son d'Aix,* a small, diamond-shaped, chewy delicacy made on a wafer base with ground almonds and fruit syrup, and glazed with icing sugar. Traditional *calissonniers* still make them, including La Maison du Roy René (www.calisson.com; 13 rue Gaston de Saporta; calisson boxes from €4.90; ⊙8am-4.30pm Mon-Thu, to 11am Fri).

★ Le Petit Verdot
PROVENCAL €€

(☎04 42 27 30 12; www.lepetitverdot.fr; 7 rue d'Entrecasteaux; mains €21-23; ⏰7pm-midnight Mon-Sat) It's all about hearty, honest dining here, with tabletops made out of old wine crates, and a lively chef-patron who runs the place with huge enthusiasm, happily showing how good Provençal food and wine can be. Expect dishes such as *onglet* (skirt steak) in green-pepper sauce or Pata Negra pork with mustard and honey, accompanied by great wines and seasonal veggies.

Jardin Mazarin
FRENCH €€

(☎04 28 31 08 36; www.jardinmazarin.com; 15 rue du 4 Septembre; lunch/dinner menus €23/29; ⏰9am-3pm & 7-10.30pm Mon-Sat) This elegant restaurant is set perfectly on the ground floor of a handsome 18th-century *hôtel particulier* in the Quartier Mazarin. Two salons sit beneath splendid beamed ceilings, but the real gem is the verdant fountain-centred garden, which comes into its own in summer. Expect knowledgeable treatment of local, seasonal produce (such as truffles and asparagus) from the kitchen.

★ La Table de Pierre Reboul
GASTRONOMY €€€

(☎04 42 52 27 27; www.chateaudelapioline.com; 260 rue Guillaume du Vair, Château de la Pioline; lunch/dinner menus from €51/72; ⏰noon-2pm & 7-10pm) Pierre Reboul's renowned restaurant has moved from central Aix to the aristocratic Château de la Pioline, a suitably smart location for his high-class cuisine. The rich, indulgent French fare meets flavours and ingredients cherry-picked from

✓ TOP TIP: AIX-CELLENT MARKET

At the daily food market (place Richelme; ⏰7am-noon), trestle tables groan each morning under the weight of marinated olives, goat's cheese, garlic, lavender, honey, peaches, melons, cherries and a bounty of other sun-kissed fruit, veggies and seasonal food. Plane trees provide ample shade on the atmospheric T-shaped square, endowed with a couple of corner cafes where Aixois catch up on the gossip over *un café* once their shopping is done.

across the globe (like tempura prawns, or the day's fish with goat's curd and spinach). Rooms are similarly sumptuous too (doubles from €145).

The chateau is 5km southwest of town on the D65 towards the TGV station.

Drinking & Nightlife

The scene is fun but fickle. For nightlife, hit the student-friendly drinking dens on rue de la Verrerie and place Richelme. Open-air cafes crowd the city's squares, especially Forum des Cardeurs, place de Verdun and place de l'Hôtel de Ville (our favourite, for its more intimate scale and shady trees).

La Mado
CAFE

(Chez Madeleine; ☎04 42 38 28 02; www.la-mado-aix.fr; 4 place des Prêcheurs; ⏰7am-2am) This smart cafe, with steel-grey parasols and box-hedged terrace on a busy square, is unbeatable for coffee and fashionable-people watching. Its European food, a wide range of tartares, pastas, fish and meat (plat du jour €17, *menus* €24-38) is augmented by very decent sushi.

🛍 Shopping

Chic fashion boutiques cluster along pedestrian rue Marius Reynaud and cours Mirabeau. But it is at the daily morning market on place Richelme, piled high with marinated olives, goat-milk cheese, lavender, honey, fruit and a bounty of other seasonal foods, that you'll find the local Aixois crowd. Or try the Sunday-morning flower market on place des Prêcheurs.

★ Book in Bar
BOOKS

(☎04 42 26 60 07; www.bookinbar.com; 4 rue Joseph Cabassol; ⏰9am-7pm Mon-Sat) Bibliophiles rejoice: this brilliant Anglophile bookshop has a huge selection of English-language books for sale (among works in other languages) and a thoroughly pleasant tearoom to boot. Look out for occasional book readings, jazz evenings and an English-language book club on the last Thursday of the month (from 5.30pm).

La Chambre aux Confitures
FOOD

(☎04 42 24 07 74; www.lachambreauxconfitures. com; 16bis rue d'Italie; ⏰10am-2pm & 3-7pm Mon-

WORTH A TRIP: A QUINTESSENTIAL PROVENÇAL LUNCH

The delightful hilltop village of Ventabren lies 15km west of Aix-en-Provence, providing a perfect lazy day trip. It's the gorgeous medieval town itself, built as protection from Saracen raids from the 10th century, that's the attraction – but the perfect way to conclude a day exploring its narrow, cobbled lanes is to dine at La Table de Ventabren (☑ 04 42 28 79 33; www.danb.fr; 1 rue Frédéric Mistral; menus €48-107; ☺ kitchen noon-1.15pm & 7.45-9.15pm Tue-Sun May-Sep, shorter hours rest of year). Many restaurants with stunning views rest on their laurels in the kitchen: not so La Table de Ventabren. This Michelin-starred restaurant – with a canvas-canopied terrace that's nothing short of magical on summer evenings – serves exquisite food. Chef Dan Bessoudo creates inventive French dishes and out-of-this-world desserts.

Fri, to 7.30pm Sat, to 1pm Sun) This pretty, orderly little shop sells delicious artisanal jams – including unexpected flavours like gooseberry, lavender, strawberries in champagne and bitter lemon – and other condiments for cheese and charcuterie. They're happy for you to mix-and-match and create your own gift packs.

ⓘ Information

Tourist Office (☑ 04 42 16 11 61; www. aixenprovencetourism.com; 300 av Giuseppe Verdi, Les Allées; ☺ 8.30am-7pm Mon-Sat, 10am-1pm & 2-6pm Sun Apr-Sep, 8.30am-6pm Mon-Sat Oct-Mar; ☏) Touch screens add a high-tech edge to the usual collection of brochures at this tourist office. Sells tickets for guided tours and cultural events, and has a shop selling regional souvenirs.

ARLES & THE CAMARGUE

Arles

POP 52,886

Roman treasures, shady squares and plenty of Camarguais culture make Arles a seductive stepping stone into the Camargue. And if its colourful sun-baked houses evoke a sense of déjà vu, it's because you've seen them already on a Van Gogh canvas – the artist painted 200-odd works around town, though sadly his famous little 'yellow house' at 2 place Lamartine, which he painted in 1888, was destroyed during WWII.

Arles' Saturday market is also a must-see – it's one of Provence's best.

◉ Sights

★ **Les Arènes** ROMAN SITE
(Amphithéâtre; ☑ 08 91 70 03 70; www.arenes-arles. com; Rond-Point des Arènes; adult/child €6/free, incl Théâtre Antique €9/free; ☺ 9am-8pm Jul & Aug, to 7pm May, Jun & Sep, shorter hours Oct-Apr) In Roman Gaul, every important town had an amphitheatre, where gladiators and wild animals met their (usually grisly) ends. Few examples have survived, but Arles (like nearby Nîmes) has preserved its colosseum largely intact. At 136m long, 107m wide and 21m tall, built around AD 90, the oval-shaped amphitheatre would have held 21,000 baying spectators. Though the structure has suffered down the centuries, it's still evocative of the might and capabilities of Roman civilisation. Entry is on the northern side.

★ **Fondation Vincent Van Gogh** GALLERY
(☑ 04 90 93 08 08; www.fondation-vincentvangogh-arles.org; 35ter rue du Docteur Fanton; adult/child €9/free; ☺ 10am-7pm Jul & Aug, from 11am Sep-Jun) Housed in a listed 15th-century manor, now twice repurposed (its other incarnation was as a bank), this Van Gogh–themed gallery is a must-see, as much for the architecture as the art. It has no permanent collection – rather, it hosts one or two excellent exhibitions a year, always with a Van Gogh theme and always including at least one Van Gogh masterpiece. Architectural highlights include the rooftop terrace and the coloured-glass bookshop ceiling. Look online for child- and family-centred programs.

★ **Musée Réattu** GALLERY
(☑ 04 90 49 37 58; www.museereattu.arles.fr; 10 rue du Grand Prieuré; adult/child €8/free; ☺ 10am-6pm Tue-Sun, to 5pm Dec-Feb) This superb 150-year-old

Arles

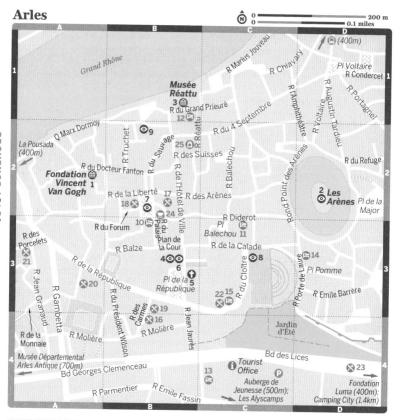

Arles

museum, housed in an exquisitely renovated 15th-century Hospitaller priory by the Rhône, might be assumed old-fashioned, yet its modern collection is truly top-notch. Among its holdings are works by 18th- and 19th-century Provençal artists, two paintings and 57 sketches by Picasso, and of course some works from its namesake, Jacques Réattu. It also stages wonderfully curated cutting-edge exhibitions.

Musée Départemental Arles Antique
MUSEUM

(🖉 04 13 31 51 03; www.arles-antique.cg13.fr; av de la Première Division Française Libre; adult/child €8/free; ⊙10am-6pm Wed-Mon; 🅿) This striking cobalt-blue museum perches on the edge of what used to be the Roman chariot-racing track (hippodrome), southwest of central Arles. The collection of pagan and Christian finds includes stunning mosaics and an entire wing of treasures highlighting Arles' commercial and maritime prominence. Permanent collections reach back to prehistory, through the arrival of the Greeks in 600 BC to the Roman period and beyond. If you love a proper museum, full of artefacts and history, this is for you.

Théâtre Antique
ROMAN SITE

(🖉 04 90 49 59 05; rue de la Calade; adult/child, incl entry to Les Arènes, €9/free; ⊙9am-7pm May-Sep, to 6pm Mar, Apr & Oct, 10am-5pm Nov-Feb) It's easy to admire the grace and engineering of this theatre – built at the behest of the unofficial first Roman Emperor, Augustus, in the 1st century BC, despite a semi-ruinous state brought on by centuries of pilfering. It still serves as one of Arles' premier venues, staging summertime concerts and plays where lighting, seating for 10,000 and the few remaining pillars create a magical atmosphere. The entrance and ticket office is on rue de la Calade.

Cryptoportiques
ROMAN SITE

(place de la République, Hôtel de Ville; adult/child €4.50/free; ⊙10am-5pm Nov-Feb, 9am-6pm Mar, Apr & Oct,to 7pm May-Sep) The origins of these fascinating underground chambers, now sitting below the current city centre, go at least back to the first Roman colony in Arles in 46 BC, and most likely extend to much older Greek caverns. It's a wonderfully literal 2000-year excursion to take the stairs from the gleaming administrative heart of modern Arles, down to three vaulted chambers that may have housed shops or storage cellars under the Roman forum.

Les Alyscamps
CEMETERY

(av des Alyscamps; adult/child €4.50/free; ⊙9am-7pm May-Sep, shorter hours rest of year) Testament to the significance of Roman Arles, this grand processional avenue of tombs and sarcophagi holds more than 1500 years of corpses (which Roman custom insisted were buried outside the city). Van Gogh and Gauguin both painted this necropolis, at the eastern end of which stands the marvellously atmospheric, unfinished 11th-century St-Honorat chapel.

Église St-Trophime
CHURCH

(6 place de la République; ⊙8am-noon & 2-6pm Mon, Fri & Sat, to 5pm Tue-Thu, 2-5pm Sun) Named for Arles' semi-mythical first archbishop, this Romanesque-style church, built over a 5th-century basilica, was a cathedral until the bishopric moved to Aix in 1801. Built between the 12th and 15th centuries, it's considered a masterpiece of Provençal Romanesque. Look for the intricately sculpted western portal, topped by a tympanum depicting the Apocalypse (and St Trophime himself, brandishing his crozier). Inside, the treasury contains bone fragments of Arles' bishops. Occasional exhibitions are hosted in neighbouring cloister, Cloître St-Trophime.

Tickets to exhibitions in the cloister are sold at the town hall or the tourist office.

🎉 Festivals & Events

Fête des Gardians
CULTURAL

(⊙1 May) Mounted *gardians* (Camarguais cowboys) parade and hold games in central Arles during this festival, which affords a fascinating insight into the region's traditions. The show, put on by the Brotherhood of the Gardians, founded in 1512, culminates in the Arena d'Arles.

INFO: CENT SAVER

Buy a pass for multiple sights at the Arles tourist office or any Roman site: the Pass Avantage (€16) covers the museums, both theatres, the baths, crypt, Les Alyscamps and the Cloître St-Trophime; the Pass Liberté (€12) gives you the choice of a total of six sights, including two museums.

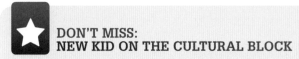

DON'T MISS:
NEW KID ON THE CULTURAL BLOCK

Arles' already-bulging cultural landscape avidly awaits Fondation Luma (☑ 04 90 47 76 17; www.luma-arles.org; 45 chemin des Minimes; ☺ Parc des Ateliers 11am-6pm Wed-Sun), a new cutting-edge gallery and arts centre, rising inexorably at a defunct railway depot in the city's southeastern quarter. Funded by the Swiss-based Luma Foundation, and designed by Frank Gehry, it's set for a high-profile opening in 2019. If you want a scoop, there are French-language guided visits of the site five times a week, and one in English at 11.30am on Saturdays (adult/child €7/free).

Fêtes d'Arles   CULTURAL
(www.festivarles.com; ☺ mid-Jun–early Jul) Races, parades, costumes, theatre and music come to Arles over several weeks from mid-June. Highlights include La Course de Satin – a bareback race on pure-bred Camargue horses dating from 1529 – and the Pegoulado – a torchlight procession of participants dressed in traditional Provençal costume that has wended its way through town to the Roman theatre since at least 1830.

Les Suds   MUSIC
(☑ 04 90 96 06 27; www.suds-arles.com; ☺ Jul) This wonderfully imaginative and multifaceted world-music festival makes use of Arles venues as diverse as the Roman theatre and the abandoned industrial complex Parc des Ateliers. While the main festival occurs over a week in July, the organisers stay busy throughout the year with live events, workshops and more.

Les Rencontres d'Arles Photographie   ART
(www.rencontres-arles.com; adult/child from €28/23; ☺ Jul-Sep) This internationally renowned photography festival, with a pedigree stretching to 1969, makes great use of a number of heritage sites around Arles for its many exhibits, debates, performances and workshops.

🛏 Sleeping

Camping City   CAMPGROUND €
(☑ 04 90 93 08 86; www.camping-city.com; 67 rte de Crau; 1-/2-person sites €18/20; ☺ Apr-Sep; P ⛌) On the road to Marseille, 1.5km southeast of town, Camping City is the closest campground to Arles. Bike hire and laundry facilities are available, and there are indoor and outdoor activities for kids. To get here, take bus 2 to the Hermite stop.

Auberge de Jeunesse   HOSTEL €
(☑ 04 90 96 18 25; www.hifrance.org; 20 av Maréchal Foch; dm incl breakfast & linen €20.30; ☺ Mar-Oct) Modern, shiny and neat, this efficient if uninspiring hostel's drawcard is its location, 10 minutes' walk from the city centre. The usual Fédération Unie des Auberges de Jeunesse (FUAJ) facilities are on offer – kitchen, lounge, cafe and dorms of varying sizes, plus a bar. Bedding is provided, towels aren't, and the doors are locked at 11pm.

La Pousada   B&B €€
(☑ 06 74 44 39 77; www.lapousada.net; 9 rue Croix Rouge; s/d €90/116; ☺ Mar-Nov; ✻ @ 🖥) Down by the Rhône, this relaxed B&B offers three rustic-chic rooms, all named after spices, with admirable details like brass sinks, open-plan showers and sparkly tiled floors. The complimentary breakfast can be taken in the walled garden in fine weather, and there are bikes and books to borrow.

Le Calendal   HOTEL €€
(☑ 04 90 96 11 89; www.lecalendal.com; 5 rue Porte de Laure; s/d/tr €109/149/159; ☺ lunch noon-2.30pm, salon de thé 4-6pm; ✻ 🖥) Hotel, spa and restaurant, this cosy bolthole opposite the Théâtre Antique has bright rooms and an inviting stone-walled garden. Breakfast is a buffet in Le Comptoir du Calendal (mains €12-18; ☺ 8am-8.30pm; 🖥). A massage in the spa is always a good idea.

Hôtel de l'Amphithéâtre   HISTORIC HOTEL €€
(☑ 04 90 96 10 30; www.hotelamphitheatre.fr; 5-7 rue Diderot; s/d €89/109; ✻ @ 🖥) This elegant address across from the amphitheatre is quite a bargain: the standard of design here far outreaches the reasonable price tag. Antiques, rugs, fireplaces and staircases speak of the building's history, while minimal rooms nod to modern trends, and several have super views over Les Arènes and Arles' rooftops (although you'll pay for the privilege).

Hôtel du Musée
BOUTIQUE HOTEL €€

(☑ 04 90 93 88 88; www.hoteldumusee.com; 11 rue du Grand Prieuré; s/d from €80/110; ❉ 🛜) In a sensitively preserved 16th- to 17th-century building, this impeccable hotel has 28 peaceful rooms decorated with simple, high-quality furnishings, a chequerboard-tiled breakfast room (breakfast €9.50) and a patio garden brimming with pretty blossoms. Perhaps inspired by the proximity of so many world-class museums, it also has a small exhibition room. Parking is €15 per night.

⭐ Hôtel Jules César
DESIGN HOTEL €€€

(☑ 04 90 52 52 52; www.hotel-julescesar.fr; 9 bd des Lices; r from €226; ❉🛜🏊) It's not often you can say you've stayed somewhere designed from scratch by a world-famous fashion icon – but that's what you get at this luxe address (part of Sofitel's MGallery collection), renovated by couturier Christian Lacroix. Once a convent for Carmelite nuns, it's now a temple to fashion, glittering with over-the-top mirrors, Roman busts, modern art and trendy textiles.

⭐ Le Cloître
DESIGN HOTEL €€€

(☑ 04 88 09 10 00; www.hotelducloitre.com; 18 rue du Cloître; r €213; ❉@🛜) The traditional Mediterranean courtyard that greets you on arrival at 'The Cloister' is charming enough, but doesn't betray the inventiveness of the warm, colourful design within. Its 19 rooms are all distinct, with Italian showers and unusual furniture that sacrifices no comfort.

Rooms are €14 per person cheaper if you forgo breakfast, and there's a panoramic rooftop terrace.

🍴 Eating

Arles and its environs are foodie heaven; reserve ahead. Places often close between 3pm and 6pm, and hours are reduced in winter.

⭐ Marché d'Arles
MARKET €

(☑ 04 90 49 36 36; bd des Lices; ⊙ 8am-1pm Sat) Plan to be in Arles for the whopping Saturday morning market. You'll find all of Camargue's best produce: salt, rice, goat's cheese, *saucisson d'Arles* (bull-meat sausage) and so much more. Stalls line both sides of the street as visitors and locals alike browse, sample and buy everything from lavender honey to baby chicks.

Glacier Arlelatis
ICE CREAM €

(☑ 06 50 05 74 39; 8 place du Forum; 1/2 scoops €2/4; ⊙12.30-11pm) Thirty-eight flavours of artisanal ice cream and sorbet are the mainstays of this *glacier* on busy place du Forum. Buy a cone to take away or treat yourself to a magnificent whipped-cream-topped sundae sitting down. Flavours change but there are always a few distinctly Provençal ones: lavender honey, chestnut and so forth.

Fadoli et Fadola
CAFE €

(☑ 04 90 49 70 73; 44 rue des Arènes; sandwiches €5, salads €7; ⊙noon-2.30pm; 🍴) Well-stuffed

ROMEOFOTO/SHUTTERSTOCK ©

Market, Arles

sandwiches – made to order, *frotté à l'ail* (rubbed with garlic) and dripping with silken AOC Vallée des Baux olive oil – lure the crowds to this tiny sandwich shop with a hole-in-the-wall takeaway counter. It also sells olive oil by the litre (€12 to €25) and even sushi. Find it footsteps from central 'cafe' square, place du Forum.

★ **Le Gibolin** BISTRO €€
(☑ 04 88 65 43 14; 13 rue des Porcelets; 2-/3-course menus €27/34; ⌚ 12.15-2pm & 8-10.30pm Tue-Sat Apr-Jul & Oct, shorter hours rest of year) After spending three decades plying Paris with their passion for organic wines, owners Brigitte and Luc decided to head south and do the same for Arles. Unsurprisingly, it's become a much-loved local fixture, known for its hearty home cooking and peerless wine list (racked up temptingly behind the bar and mostly available by the glass).

★ **L'Autruche** MODERN FRENCH €€
(☑ 04 90 49 73 63; 5 rue Dulau; menus €29; ⌚ noon-1.30pm & 7.30-9pm Thu-Sun, noon-1.30pm Wed)

'The Ostrich', run by husband-and-wife team Fabien and Ouria, is a family restaurant in the best tradition. Market-fresh produce is assured, as is the ability of their Michelin-experienced chef to treat it with skill – perhaps plaice with cocoa beans or silky asparagus soup with nuts. Extravagant desserts are a further treat.

L'Ouvre Boîte TAPAS €€
(☑ 04 88 09 10 10; 22 rue du Cloître; dishes €8-10; ⌚ 6.30-9.30pm Mon-Fri, 11am-2pm & 6.30-9.30pm Sat & Sun) Alexandre's little joint (the 'Open Box') has become a firm Arlésian favourite for chilled evening eats in the courtyard of the Hôtel du Cloître. It specialises in shared tapas-like 'little plates' – oysters, octopus in herby-tomato sauce, pork in Asian broth – ordered to share. Arrive early for a prime table.

★ **L'Atelier Jean-Luc Rabanel** GASTRONOMY €€€
(☑ 04 90 91 07 69; www.rabanel.com; 7 rue des Carmes; menus €55-155; ⌚ noon-1pm & 8-9pm Thu-

VINCENT VAN GOGH

It's easy to forget that Vincent van Gogh was only 37 when he died, as he appears much older in some of his self-portraits. Born in 1853, the Dutch painter arrived in Arles in 1888 after living in Paris with his younger brother Theo, an art dealer who financially supported Vincent from his own modest income. In Paris he had become acquainted with seminal artists Edgar Degas, Camille Pissarro, Henri de Toulouse-Lautrec and Paul Gauguin.

Revelling in Arles' intense light and bright colours, Van Gogh painted with a burning fervour, unfazed by howling mistral winds. During a mistral he would kneel on his canvases and paint horizontally, or lash his easel to iron stakes driven deep into the ground. He sent paintings to Theo for him to try to sell, and dreamed of founding an artists' colony in Arles, but only Gauguin accepted his invitation. Their differing artistic approaches (Gauguin believed in painting from imagination, Van Gogh in painting what he saw) and artistic temperaments came to a head with the argument in December 1888 that led to Van Gogh lopping off part of his own ear.

In May 1889 Van Gogh voluntarily entered an asylum, Monastère St-Paul de Mausole (p77) in St-Rémy de Provence. During his one year, one week and one day's confinement he painted 150-odd canvases, including masterpieces like *Starry Night* (not to be confused with *Starry Night over the Rhône*, painted in Arles).

In February 1890 Van Gogh's Arles-painted work *The Red Vines* (1888) was bought by Anne Boch, sister of his friend Eugene Boch, for 400 francs (around €50 today) – the only painting he sold in his lifetime. It now hangs in the Pushkin State Museum of Fine Arts.

On 16 May 1890 Van Gogh moved to Auvers-sur-Oise, just outside Paris, to be closer to Theo. But on 27 July that year he shot himself and died two days later, with Theo at his side. Theo subsequently had a breakdown, was committed and died, aged 33, just six months after Vincent. Less than a decade later, Van Gogh's talent started to achieve recognition, with major museums acquiring his work.

Sat, noon-1pm Sun, 8-9pm Wed) As much an artistic experience as a double-Michelin-starred adventure, this is the gastronomic flagship of charismatic chef Jean-Luc Rabanel. Many products are sourced from the chef's veggie patch, and wine pairings are an experience in themselves. Saturday-morning cooking classes are also available, working with the kitchen brigade (€200). Next door, Rabanel's À Côté (☑ 04 90 47 61 13; www.bistro-acote.com; 21 rue des Carmes; menus €32; ⊙ noon-1.30pm & 7.30-9pm Wed-Sun) offers bistro fare.

🍷 Drinking & Nightlife

Le Café Van Gogh CAFE
(Le Café La Nuit; ☑ 04 90 96 44 56; www.restaurant-cafe-van-gogh.com; 11 place du Forum; ⊙ 11am-3pm & 6-11pm) Immortalised in Van Gogh's 1888 *Terrasse du Café le Soir*, this cafe trades on its plum spot on the place du Forum and its association with the adopted Arlésian painter. Shaded by plane trees, it turns into a giant terrace at lunch and dinner during summer.

La Guinguette du Patio de Camargue LIVE MUSIC
(☑ 04 90 49 51 76; www.chico.fr; 49 chemin de Barriol; ⊙ 11am-midnight) Established in 1995 by Chico, co-founder of the Gypsy Kings, on a patch of industrial wasteland by the banks of the Rhône, this is now a wonderful riverside grill and bar. When the weather's good, it can be very festive, especially if the owner's new band, Chico and the Gypsies, are in a musical mood. Check the site for 'dinner concerts'.

🛍 Shopping

La Boutique des Passionnés MUSIC
(☑ 04 90 96 59 93; www.passionnes.com; 14 rue Réattu; ⊙ 9am-7pm Tue-Sat) Starting out as a humble record shop, La Boutique des Passionnés has grown into a cultural centre – promoting and selling tickets for shows, hosting intimate performances of Iberian music, selling literature and sculptures, and booking author signings and exhibitions. It's a friendly and important part of Arles' cultural scene.

ℹ Information

Tourist Office (☑ 04 90 18 41 20; www. arlestourisme.com; 9 blvd des Lices; ⊙ 9am-

FÉRIA D'ARLES

While it unavoidably centres on the ethically questionable 'sport' of bullfighting, the Féria d'Arles is also unavoidably one of the highlights of the city's calendar. Or rather, two of them: one in Easter marking the beginning of the bullfighting season, and one in September, called the Féria du Riz (Festival of Rice), but also involving bullfighting.

Over half a million visitors and bullfighting aficionados descend on Arles for the Easter Féria, with 50,000 cramming into the Roman amphitheatre Les Arènes to see the fights (and the less cruel bull-leaping). But it's in the streets of Arles that the true Féria unfurls: music, feasting, parties, traditional costumes and instruments are all abundant.

6.45pm Apr-Sep, to 4.45pm Mon-Sat, 10am-1pm Sun Oct-Mar;)

ℹ Getting Around

1Véloc (☑ 04 86 32 27 05; www.1veloc.fr; 12 rue de la Cavalerie; bike/ebike per day from €8/25; ⊙ 10am-12.30pm & 3-6pm Tue-Fri, 3-6pm Sat Sep-Jun, plus 10am-noon & 5-6pm Sun Jul & Aug) Rents out bikes and runs tours.

Camargue Wetlands

Travelling around the Camargue is tantamount to frolicking with a zillion mosquitoes in a giant nature park. Almost all the Camargue's wetlands are protected by the 863-sq-km Parc Naturel Régional de Camargue, created to preserve its fragile ecosystems by maintaining an equilibrium between ecological considerations and economic mainstays: agriculture, salt and rice production, hunting, grazing and tourism. Pick up information on walking, birdwatching and other activities at the park-run Musée de la Camargue (p72).

On the periphery, the 600-sq-km lagoon Étang de Vaccarès and nearby peninsulas and islands form the 135-sq-km Réserve Nationale de Camargue (☑ 04 90 97 00 97; www.reserve-camargue.org; C134, rte de Fiélouse, La Capelière). Get the full low-down on the

Wild white horses, the Carmargue

reserve and its activities at the information centre (p46) in La Capelière.

The Camargue's two largest towns are the seaside pilgrim's outpost Stes-Maries-de-la-Mer and, to the northwest, the walled town of Aigues-Mortes.

👁 Sights

Musée de la Camargue   MUSEUM
(Musée Camarguais; ☎04 90 97 10 82; www.parc-camargue.fr; D570, Mas du Pont de Rousty; adult/child €5/free; ⊗9am-12.30pm & 1-6pm Apr-Sep, 10am-5.30pm Oct-Mar) Inside a 19th-century sheep shed 10km southwest of Arles, this museum evokes traditional life in the Camargue, with exhibitions covering history, culture, ecosystems, farming techniques, flora and fauna. *L'Oeuvre Horizons* by Japanese artist Tadashi Kawamata – aka a wooden observatory shaped like a boat – provides a bird's-eye view of the agricultural estate, which is crossed by a 3.5km walking trail. The headquarters of the Parc Naturel Régional de Camargue (PNRC; www.parc-camargue.fr) is also based here.

★ Domaine de la Palissade   PARK
(☎04 42 86 81 28; www.palissade.fr; 36 chemin Départemental; adult/child €3/free, horse trekking per hour adult/child from €19/16; ⊗9am-6pm mid-Jun–mid-Sep, to 5pm Mar–mid-Jun & mid-Sep–Oct, 9am-5pm Wed-Sun Feb & Nov; Ⓟ) This remote nature centre, 12km south of Salin de Gi-

raud, organises fantastic forays through 702 hectares of protected marshland, scrubby glasswort, flowering sea lavender (in August) and lagoons on foot and horseback (call ahead to book horse treks). Before hitting the scrub, rent binoculars (€2) and grab a free map of the estate's three marked walking trails (1km to 8km) from the office. The tours are as educational as they are enjoyable.

Cabanes de Cacharel   HORSE RIDING
(☎04 90 97 84 10, 06 11 57 74 75; www.cabanes decacharel.com; rte de Cacharel, D85A; horse trek per hour/day €22/70) Farms along rte d'Arles offer *promenades à cheval* (horseback riding) astride white Camargue horses, but this stable, just north of Stes-Maries-de-la-Mer along the parallel rte de Cacharel (D85A), offer more involved and memorable treks. They also offer one-hour horse-and-carriage rides (€18) and tours where you get to experience the life of a traditional *gardian* (Camargue cowboy).

La Maison du Guide   OUTDOORS
(☎04 66 73 52 30, 06 12 44 73 52; www.maison duguide.camargue.fr; 154 rue du Château de Montcalm, Montcalm; guided tours adult/child €20/free, 4-person cottage per week €270-550; ⊗office 9am-noon Mon; ♿) Discovery weekends by naturalist Jean-Marie Espuche embrace birdwatching, cycling, horse riding and sunrise nature walks. You'll find 'secret'

parts of the Camargue and see much more birdlife than you otherwise might. Jean-Marie also rents out a four-person cottage in Montcalm, a useful base on the edge of the Camargue.

- - - - - - - - - - - - - - - -

🛏 Sleeping

The most obvious base in the Camargue is Arles, which has a wealth of accommodation. Further out into the countryside hotels are less sophisticated, but there are some attractive B&Bs, cabins and rural campgrounds scattered around.

Ranch-style motel accommodation lines the D570 heading into Stes-Maries-de-la-Mer. The tourist offices can point you towards self-catering *cabanes de gardian* (traditional whitewashed cowboy cottages) and farmstays.

★ Le Mas de Peint   BOUTIQUE HOTEL €€€
(📞04 90 97 20 62; www.masdepeint.com; rte de Salin de Giraud, Le Sambuc, Manade Jacques Bon; d €250; ⊙mid-Mar–mid-Nov; ❋🅿🛜🏊) This 17th-century farmhouse has managed to become an upmarket hotel without jettisoning design elements that nod to its rural roots: solid beams, wooden furniture, saddles on the walls, and a bull's head in the lobby. But it's the superb restaurant (menus lunch €39, dinner €41-69; ⊙lunch & dinner Sat & Sun, lunch only Fri & Mon-Wed) many come for – watch chefs work from the dining room, or eat on the lovely poolside terrace.

★ Mas de Calabrun   HOTEL €€€
(📞04 90 97 82 21; www.mas-de-calabrun.fr; rte de Cacherel, D85A; s/d/wagons €167/199/185; ⊙mid-Feb–mid-Nov; 🅿@🛜🏊) From the striking equestrian sculpture in its front courtyard to the swish pool, stylish restaurant terrace and fabulous views of open Camargue countryside, this hotel thoroughly deserves its three stars. There are 31 individually designed rooms, but the icing on the cake is the trio of *roulottes* (old-fashioned 'gypsy' wagons), which promise the perfect romantic getaway. Breakfast is €15.

- - - - - - - - - - - - - - - -

🍴 Eating

★ Le Mazet du Vaccarès   SEAFOOD €€
(Chez Hélène et Néné; 📞04 90 97 10 79; www.mazet-du-vaccares.fr; rte Albaron Villeneuve; fish/bouillabaisse menu €38/60; ⊙10am-11pm Fri-Sun

mid-Jan–mid-Aug & mid-Sep–mid-Dec; 🅿) Shuddering along the low ribbed road past flamingos and Camargue ponies is totally worth it for the seafood at this legendary lakeside cabin. Memorabilia from Hélène and Néné's days as lighthouse keepers in Beauduc fill the restaurant with soul. The jovial couple cook up one fixed *menu,* built from the catch of local fishers. They accept cash only.

★ La Telline   FRENCH €€
(📞04 90 97 01 75; www.restaurantlatelline.fr; Quarter Villeneuve, rte de Gageron, Villeneuve; mains €24-35; ⊙noon-1.15pm & 7.30-9pm Thu-Mon; 🅿) A true local favourite, this isolated cottage restaurant with sage-green wooden shutters is one of the best places to sample genuine Camargue food. Summer dining is in a small and peaceful flower-filled garden, where straightforward starters such as *tellines* (molluscs), salad or terrine are followed by grilled fish or meat, or a beef or bull steak. No credit cards.

The owners also run several *chambres d'hôtes* (doubles from €115).

Chez Bob   FRENCH €€
(📞04 90 97 00 29; www.restaurantbob.fr; Mas Petite Antonelle, rte du Sambuc, Villeneuve; menu €45; ⊙noon-2pm & 7.30-9pm Wed-Sun; 🅿) This house restaurant is an iconic address adored by Arlésians. Feast on grilled bull chops, mullet eggs and *anchoïade* (a powerful Provençal garlic and anchovy emulsion) beneath trees or inside between walls plastered in photos, posters and other memorabilia collected over the years by Jean-Guy, aka 'Bob'. It's 18km south of Arles; reserve ahead.

★ La Chassagnette   GASTRONOMY €€€
(📞04 90 97 26 96; www.chassagnette.fr; rte du Sambuc, Domaine de L'Armellière; menus €55-115; ⊙noon-1.30pm & 7-9.30pm Jun-Sep, noon-1.30pm Thu-Sat Oct-May; 🅿) Surrounded by a vast *potager* (kitchen garden), which supplies practically all the restaurant's produce, this renowned gourmet table is run by Armand Amal, a former pupil of Alain Ducasse. The multicourse *menus* are full of surprises, and the bucolic setting is among the loveliest anywhere in the Camargue. There's a vegetarian *menu* (unfortunately available only at lunch).

Stes-Maries-de-la-Mer

POP 2680

The saints who give their name to this whitewashed seaside town are Marie-Salomé and Marie-Jacobé, persecuted early Christians who escaped here from Palestine. With them, the legend says, was their hand-maiden Sara, whose sanctification as Saint Sara the Black makes this a significant place of pilgrimage for Roma and other 'gypsy' peoples, whose patron she is. Stes-Maries has a rough-and-tumble holidaymaker feel, with salt-licked buildings crowding dusty streets. During its Roma pilgrimages, street-cooked pans of paella fuel chaotic crowds of carnivalesque guitarists, dancers and mounted cowboys.

◉ Sights & Activities

Stes-Maries-de-la-Mer is fringed by 30km of fine-sand beaches, easily reached by bicycle. Nudist beaches surround the Gacholle light-house off the Digue à la Mer.

Église des Stes-Maries   CHURCH

(☎04 90 97 80 25; www.sanctuaire-des-saintes maries.fr; 2 place de l'Église; rooftop €2.50; ⊗10am-noon & 2-5pm Mon-Sat, 2-5pm Sun) Built on the potential first site of Christianity in the Ca-margue, this fortified church is of uncertain vintage, but probably hails from the 12th century. It draws legions of pilgrims to ven-erate the statue of Sara, their revered patron saint, during the Pèlerinage des Gitans (Roma pilgrimages; ⊗24-25 May). The relics of Sara and those of Marie-Salomé and Marie-Jacobé, all found in the crypt by King René in 1448, are enshrined in a wooden chest, stashed in the stone wall above the choir. Don't miss the panorama from the rooftop terrace.

★ Parc Ornithologique
du Pont de Gau   WILDLIFE RESERVE

(☎04 90 97 82 62; www.parcornithologique.com; D570, Pont du Gau; adult/child €7.50/5; ⊗9am-7pm Apr-Sep, 10am-6pm Oct-Mar; ⓟ⯐) Flamingos are a dime a dozen in the Camargue, but this park is one of the best places to see the many other migratory and seasonal species that thrive in these wetlands. Herons, storks, egrets, teals, avocets and grebes are just some you may spot, depending on the time of year. The reserve has 7km of trails, giving you every chance to see its avian inhabit-ants, and a care centre for sick and injured

birds. Follow the D570 4km north from Stes-Maries-de-la-Mer.

La Digue à la Mer   NATURAL FEATURE

This 2.5m-high dyke was built in the 19th century to cut the delta off from the sea, making the southern Camargue arable. A 20km-long walking and cycling track runs along its length, linking Stes-Maries with the solar-powered Phare de la Gacholle (1882), a lighthouse automated in the 1960s. Foot-paths cut down to lovely sandy beaches and views of pink flamingos strutting across the marshy planes are second to none. Walking on the fragile sand dunes is forbidden, as is driving.

Manade des Baumelles   FARM

(☎04 90 97 84 14; www.manadedesbaumelles.fr; D38; tour with/without lunch €45/25; ⊗tours 10.30am Tue-Sun; ⓟ) Located on the Petit Rhône, this manade (bull farm) lets visitors enter the world of the gardians ('cowboys'), watching their strenuous work from the safety of a truck. The braver can ride horses, join in the farm-work, go canoeing and play traditional gardian games. Tours end with an optional farm lunch (menus €25/37) and a gift shop stocked with Camargue specialities.

Find the manade a few kilometres north of Stes-Maries-de-la-Mer, at the end of a grav-el track off the D38 towards Aigues-Mortes.

Le Vélo Saintois   CYCLING

(☎04 90 97 74 56; www.levelosaintois.camargue. fr; 19 rue de la République; per day adult/child/ ebike €15/14/30; ⊗9am-7pm Mar-Nov) This bike-rental outlet has bikes of all sizes, in-cluding tandems and kids' wheels. Helmets cost an extra €1 per day. A free brochure de-tails four circular cycling itineraries (26km to 44km, four hours to eight hours) starting in Stes-Maries-de-la-Mer. Free hotel delivery.

Le Vélociste   CYCLING

(☎04 90 97 83 26; www.levelociste.fr; 8 place Mireille; per day adult/child/ebike €15/14/30; ⊗9am-7pm Mar-Nov) This bike-rental shop rents wheels, advises on cycling itineraries (24km to 70km, four hours to nine hours) and organises fun one-day combined cycling and horse-riding (from €30) or cycling and canoeing (€30) packages. Free hotel delivery.

Boating

The marshy Camargue lends itself to explo-ration by boat. Several companies (offer-ing 90-minute trips) including Les Quatre

Maries ([☎]04 90 97 70 10; www.bateaux-4maries.
camargue.fr; 36bis av Théodore Aubanel; adult/child
€12/6; [◷]mid-Mar–Oct; [♿]) and Le Camargue
([☎]06 17 95 81 96; www.bateau-camargue.com; 5
rue des Launes; adult/child €13/7; [◷]mid-Mar–Oct)
have ticketing desks along rue Théodore Aubanel, the promenade linking the town centre with Port Gardian. Further west past the
pleasure port, next to Camping Le Clos du
Rhône, is Tiki III ([☎]04 90 97 81 68; www.tiki3.fr;
chemin du Clos du Rhone, off D38; adult/child €13/7;
[◷]mid-Mar–Oct), a paddle boat moored at the
mouth of the Petit Rhône.

- -

[🛏] Sleeping

Camping Le
Clos du Rhône   CAMPGROUND €
([☎]04 90 97 85 99; www.camping-leclos.fr; rte
d'Aigues Mortes; site €30, mobile home per week
€847; [◷]late Mar–mid-Nov; [@][🛜][🏊]) Right by
the beach (yet lavishly embellished with an
onshore water park), this large and well-
equipped campground sports a range of
accommodation options: tent sites, wooden
chalets and self-catering cottages. The pool,
two-lane water slide, and beachside spa with
jacuzzi and *hammam,* plus more mundane
services like a grocer, laundry and barbecue,
make this a family favourite.

Hôtel Méditerranée   HOTEL €
([☎]04 90 97 82 09; www.hotel-mediterranee.
camargue.fr; 4 rue Frédéric Mistral; s/d €60/74;
[◷]mid-Mar–mid-Nov; [❄]) This whitewashed
cottage hotel, festooned with an abundance
of flower pots and just steps from the sea, is
truly a steal. Its 14 rooms – three with their
own little terrace garden – are spotlessly
clean, and breakfast (€8) is served in summer on a pretty vine-covered patio garden,
complete with strawberry plants, geraniums
and other potted flowers. Bike rental costs
€15 per day.

[★]Cacharel Hotel   HOTEL €€
([☎]04 90 97 95 44; www.hotel-cacharel.com; rte de
Cacharel, D85A; s/d €151/164, horse riding per hour
€30; [@][🛜][🏊]) This isolated farmstead, 400m
down an unpaved track off the D85A just
north of Stes-Maries-de-la-Mer, perfectly
balances modern-day comforts with rural
authenticity. Photographic portraits of the
bull herder who created the hotel in 1955
(son Florian runs the three-star hotel with
much love today) give the vintage dining

room soul. Rooms sit snug in whitewashed
cottages, some overlooking the water.

Swings in the paddock, horse riding with
a *gardian* (cowboy), boules to play *pétanque,* and bags of open space make it a perfect family choice. This is Camargue living at
its most relaxing.

[★]Lodge Sainte Hélène   BOUTIQUE HOTEL €€€
([☎]04 90 97 83 29; www.lodge-saintehelene.
com; chemin Bas des Launes; d for 2 nights €626;
[❄][@][🛜][🏊]) These pearly-white terraced
cottages on a peninsula on the Etang des
Launes are prime real estate for birdwatchers and romance seekers. It's so quiet you
can hear flamingos flapping past. Each
room comes with a birdwatchers' guide and
binoculars, and owner Benoît Noel is a font
of local knowledge.

THE STORY OF THE
MARYS & GITAN
PILGRIMAGES

Catholicism first reached European
shores in what's now tiny Stes-
Maries-de-la-Mer. The stories say that
Stes Marie-Salomé and Marie-Jacobé
(and some say Mary Magdalene) fled
the Holy Land in a little boat and were
caught in a storm, drifting at sea until
washing ashore here.

Provençal and Catholic lore diverge
at this point: Catholicism relates that
Sara, patron saint of the *gitans* (Roma
people, also known as gypsies),
travelled with the two Marys on the
boat. Provençal legend says Sara was
already here and was the first person
to recognise their holiness. In 1448
skeletal remains said to belong to
Sara and the two Marys were found in
a crypt in Stes-Maries-de-la-Mer.

Gitans continue to make pilgrimages, Pèlerinage des Gitans, here on
24 and 25 May (often staying for up
to three weeks), dancing and playing
music in the streets, and parading a
statue of Sara through town. The Sunday in October closest to the 22nd
sees a second pilgrimage dedicated
to the two Stes Maries; *courses Camarguaises* are also held at this time.

FÊTE DE LA TRANSHUMANCE

Every spring throughout parts of southern France, an incredible migration known as the Transhumance (⊙May/Jun) takes place as thousands of sheep are led from the coast to the mountains to summer on alpine pastures. The journey takes about six days, and sheep, goats and donkeys block many tertiary routes to the Alps, leading to the amusement or annoyance of many a tourist.

In St-Rémy de Provence on Pentecost Monday this tradition is honoured as shepherds kitted out in traditional dress lead about 6000 sheep through St-Rémy's streets on their way to the mountains, and market-day festivities fill the town.

✕ Eating

★ Ô Pica Pica   SEAFOOD €€
(☑06 10 30 33 49; www.degustationcoquillages
-lessaintesmariesdelamer.com; 16-18 av Van Gogh;
mains €17-25; ⊙noon-3pm & 7-11pm Mar-Nov) Fish
and shellfish do not come fresher than this.
Watch them get gutted, filleted and grilled
in the 'open' glass-walled kitchen, then de-
vour your meal on the sea-facing pavement
terrace or out the back in the typically Mediterranean white-walled garden. Simplicity
is king here: plastic glasses, fish grilled *à la
plancha,* and shellfish platters. No coffee
and no credit cards.

Local specialities such as *tellines* (shellfish), *langoustines* and fresh *anchois* (anchovies) are worth choosing.

La Cabane aux Coquillages   SEAFOOD €
(☑06 10 30 33 49; 16 av Van Gogh; shellfish €8.50-
12.50; ⊙noon-3pm & 5-11pm Apr-Nov) Attached to
the excellent Ô Pica Pica restaurant, this in-
formal little *cabane* (hut) specialises, unsurprisingly, in *coquillages* (shellfish): oysters,
palourdes (clams), *coques* (cockles), and
tellines (a type of local shellfish known elsewhere in France as *pignons*). Or, you could
opt for perfectly cooked *frites* (battered
baby prawns, baby squid or anchovies) and
a very cooperative glass of wine.

La Casita   GRILL €€
(☑04 86 63 63 14; 3 rue Espelly; mains €23-26;
⊙noon-2pm & 7-9pm Wed-Sun, noon-2pm Tue Apr-
Nov) The charismatic couple who run this
unpretentious address, with cartwheels for
tables, cook up the catch of the day *à la
plancha* for eight months of the year, and
spend the other four travelling. The result is
local specialities like *tellines* and baby squid
cooked to perfection, as well as more exotic
ingredients like Pata Negra pork from Spain.

La Grange   FRENCH €€
(☑04 90 97 98 05; 23 av Frédéric Mistral; mains €16-
22, menus €19-30; ⊙noon-2pm & 6.30-10pm Mar-
Nov) If you've developed a desire to get closer
to the Camargue's bulls by eating them, then
head to the Grange, an ode to Camargue's
gardians, with bull-herding memorabilia
on the walls and plenty of *taureau* (bull
meat) on the menu. Portions are copious,
and you can begin with a Lou Gardian, the
house *apéro,* mixing white wine and peach
liqueur.

ⓘ Information

Tourist Office (☑04 90 97 82 55; www.
saintesmaries.com; 5 av Van Gogh; ⊙9am-8pm
Jul & Aug, to 7pm Apr-Jun & Sep, to 6pm Oct, to
5pm Dec-Feb & Mar)

LES ALPILLES

A silvery chain of low, jagged mountains
strung between the Rivers Durance and
Rhône, the craggy limestone peaks of Les
Alpilles rise impressively to the south of the
chic town of St-Rémy de Provence. Designated as the Parc Naturel Régional des Alpilles
in 2007, the area's hill villages are best explored by car – or better still on foot, along
one of the trails that wind among the peaks.
While you walk, look out for eagles and
Egyptian vultures soaring overhead.

Covered with scrubby *maquis* and wild
almond and olive trees, the area was immortalised by Vincent van Gogh, who created
many much-loved paintings here during the
later period of his life – especially while he
was a resident at the sanatorium of Monastère St-Paul de Mausole.

St-Rémy-de-Provence

POP 10.826

Ravishing St-Rémy is about as cultured and
chi-chi as Provence gets, and yet somehow –
and in stark contrast to some of the flashier

coastal towns (St-Tropez, we're looking at you) – it's managed to cling on to its heart and soul during the gentrification process. Built from honey-coloured stone, and centred on a lovely, plane-shaded square lined by cafes, St-Rémy is a favourite summer haunt of the jet-set – and yet, even in midsummer, it's possible to find pockets of peace and quiet along the streets of the old town.

South of town, the rugged hills of Les Alpilles rise along the horizon, and one of Provence's most impressive Roman ruins can be explored – the incredibly well-preserved ancient town of Glanum.

⊙ Sights

Pick up the free Carte St-Rémy at the first sight you visit, get it stamped, then benefit from reduced admission at St-Rémy's other sights.

★ Site Archéologique de Glanum   RUINS
(☏ 04 90 92 23 79; www.site-glanum.fr; rte des Baux-de-Provence; adult/child €7.50/free, parking €2.70; ⊙ 9.30am-6.30pm Apr-Sep, 10am-5pm Oct-Mar, closed Mon Sep-Mar) It might lack the scale and ambition of some of Provence's better-known Roman monuments, but for a glimpse into everyday life in Gaul, this ancient town has no equal. A Roman colony founded around AD 27, the remains of this once-thriving town have been excavated –

complete with baths, forum, columns, marketplace, temples and houses.

Two monuments mark the entrance, 2km south of St-Rémy – a mausoleum (from around 30 BC) and France's oldest triumphal arch, built around AD 20.

★ Monastère St-Paul de Mausole   HISTORIC SITE
(☏ 04 90 92 77 00; www.saintpauldemausole.fr; adult/child €5/free; ⊙ 9.30am-6.45pm Apr-Sep, 10.15am-5.15pm Oct-Mar, closed Jan–mid-Feb) This monastery turned asylum is famous for one of its former residents – the ever-volatile Vincent van Gogh, who admitted himself in 1889. Safe within the monastery's cloistered walls, Vincent enjoyed his most productive period, completing 150-plus drawings and around 150 paintings, including his famous *Irises*. A reconstruction of his room is open to visitors, as are a Romanesque cloister and gardens growing flowers that feature in his work.

Hôtel de Sade   MUSEUM
(☏ 04 90 92 64 04; www.hotel-de-sade.fr; 1 rue du Parage; adult/child €3.50/free; ⊙ 9.30am-1pm & 2-6pm Jun-Sep, shorter hours Oct-May) Reopened after an expensive program of renovations, this impressive Renaissance *hôtel particulier* was built in 1513 by Balthazar de Sade (ancestor of the much more notorious Marquis de Sade). Since the early 20th century it has housed the most important archaeological finds from the Roman town

Site Archéologique de Glanum

of Glanum – including an amazing array of sculptures discovered at the site, such as a striking bust of Livia, wife of Emperor Augustus, thought to have been made between AD 4 and 14.

Sleeping

★ Le Sommeil des Fées   B&B €
(☑ 04 90 92 17 66; www.angesetfees-stremy.com; 4 rue du 8 Mai 1945; incl breakfast s €55-70, d €70-90) Upstairs from La Cuisine des Anges, this cosy, colourful B&B has five rooms all named after characters from Arthurian legend, blending Provençal and Andalucian decorative details. It's bright, modern and – considering you're in St-Rémy, and that the rates include breakfast – really quite a steal.

★ Sous les Figuiers   BOUTIQUE HOTEL €€
(☑ 04 32 60 15 40; www.hotelsouslesfiguiers.com; 3 av Gabriel St-René Taillandier; d €99-191; P ✳ 🖤 🛜 ☀) 'Under The Fig Trees' nicely captures the languid, leisurely, home-away-from-home feel of this charming, country-chic house a five-minute walk from the town centre. All the rooms are decorated with great style, blending distressed wood, warm colours and ethnic textiles; some are in the main house, while others are in the gorgeous garden and have cute, private patios. Breakfast costs €15.

La Maison du Village   BOUTIQUE HOTEL €€€
(☑ 04 32 60 68 20; www.lamaisonduvillage.com; 10 rue du 8 Mai 1945; d €180-220; ✳ 🛜) The epitome of classy St-Rémy, this 1750s townhouse hotel is like a design magazine come to life. All five suites have their own eclectic decor – four of them have sitting rooms and one has a freestanding tub with a view of the village church tower. The walled garden is a bucolic setting for breakfast, and the hotel even has its own candle shop.

Eating

St-Rémy has some superb cafes and bakeries, but restaurant prices tend to be on the high side. Market day is on Wednesday and is a magnet for sightseers and locals alike.

Maison Cambillau   BAKERY €
(1 rue Carnot; fougasses & sandwiches €2.60-3; ☺ 7.30am-1.30pm & 3-7.30pm Fri-Wed) Well-stuffed *fougasse* (Provençal flatbread) and baguettes with a variety of tasty fillings

make this well-established *boulangerie* (bakery) the perfect spot to stock up on a picnic. Complete the takeaway feast with a feisty meringue, bag of nougat, nutty florentine or almond- and pistachio-studded *crousadou*.

Da Peppe   ITALIAN €
(☑ 04 90 92 11 56; 2 av Fauconnet; pizza €12-16, mains €14-22; ☺ noon-2.30pm & 7-11pm Wed-Mon; ♨) Excellent pizza and pasta with a Sicilian spin – but the wonderful rooftop terrace is the bit that seals the deal.

La Cuisine des Anges   BISTRO €€
(☑ 04 90 92 17 66; www.angesetfees-stremy.com; 4 rue du 8 Mai 1945; 2-course menu €27-29, 3-course menu €32; ☺ noon-2.30pm & 7.30-11pm Mon, Wed, Sat & Sun, 7.30-11pm Thu & Fri; ✳ 🛜) You can't really go too far wrong at the Angels' Kitchen – at least if you're looking for solid, no-nonsense Provençal cooking just like *grande-mère* would have made. Tuck into dishes like slow-cooked lamb, bream fillet, baked St-Marcellin cheese and duck pot-au-feu, and dine either in the courtyard or the stone-walled dining room. Fancy, no; flavoursome, yes.

Gus   BISTRO €€€
(☑ 04 90 90 27 61; www.gussaintremy.com; 31 bd Victor Hugo; mains from €19.50; ☺ noon-2.30pm & 7-10.30pm Tue-Sat) This bright, breezy restaurant is a favourite for the chi-chi summer crowd, and with good reason: the food is classy and the ambience is buzzy, with overtones of a Parisian street cafe. It's particularly good on seafood – big *fruits de mer* platters, lobsters and plates of oysters – but there's a blackboard of French specials too.

Shopping

★ Joël Durand   CHOCOLATE
(☑ 04 90 92 38 25; www.joeldurand-chocolatier.fr; 3 bd Victor Hugo; ☺ 9.30am-12.30pm & 2.30-7.30pm) Among France's top chocolatiers, using Provençal herbs and plants – lavender, rosemary, violet and thyme – with unexpected flavours such as Earl Grey.

L'Epicerie du Calanquet   FOOD
(☑ 04 32 62 09 01; www.moulinducalanquet.fr; 8 rue de la Commune; ☺ 9.30am-1pm & 2.30-7pm Apr-Sep, 10am-1pm & 2.30-7pm Tue-Sat Oct-Mar) A delectable grocery and fine food emporium, made out to resemble a traditional village shop, and owned by the same people who run the

Moulin à Huile du Calanquet ([☎] 04 32 60 09 50; www.moulinducalanquet.fr; vieux chemin d'Arles; ⊙ 9am-noon & 2-7pm Mon-Sat, 10am-noon & 3-6pm Sun Apr-Oct, 9am-noon & 2-6.30pm Mon-Sat Nov-Mar) outside town. Their own olive-oil range takes centre stage, of course, alongside other goodies from the area – and there are tasting sessions and events on the patio during summer.

ⓘ Information

St-Rémy Tourist Office ([☎] 04 90 92 05 22; www.saintremy-de-provence.com; place Jean Jaurès; ⊙ 9.15am-12.30pm & 2-6.30pm Mon-Sat, 10am-12.30pm Sun mid-Apr–mid-Oct, longer hours Jul & Aug, shorter hours mid-Oct–mid-Apr)

Orange

POP 30,008

Two thousand years ago, Orange – then known as Arausio – was one of the major settlements in this sunbaked corner of the Gallo-Roman empire. To cement its status, townsfolk constructed an impressive series of structures, including the town's mighty ancient theatre. Once the largest in Gaul, it still steals the show and is rightly (along with Orange's triumphal arch) a World Heritage Site. Unfortunately, despite its massive scale, the limestone structure is surprisingly fragile, and a monumental eight-year restoration project is currently under way to preserve it for the future. Expect scaffolding until at least 2024.

The modern town itself isn't quite as starry – in fact, in places it looks positively unloved – so there's no real reason to spend the night unless you have to.

⊙ Sights

★ **Théâtre Antique**   HISTORIC SITE
(Ancient Roman Theatre; [☎] 04 90 51 17 60; www.theatre-antique.com; rue Madeleine Roch; adult/child €9.50/7.50; ⊙ 9am-7pm Jun-Aug, to 6pm Apr, May & Sep, 9.30am-5.30pm Mar & Oct, 9.30am-4.30pm Nov-Feb) Orange's monumental, Unesco-protected Roman theatre is unquestionably one of France's most impressive Roman sights. It's one of only three intact Roman theatres left in the world (the others are in Syria and Turkey), and its sheer size is awe-inspiring: designed to seat 10,000 spectators, its stage wall reaches 37m high, 103m wide and 1.8m thick. Little wonder

that Louis XIV called it 'the finest wall in my kingdom'.

★ **Colline St-Eutrope**   GARDENS
For bird's-eye views of the theatre – and phenomenal vistas of Mont Ventoux and the Dentelles de Montmirail – follow montée Philbert de Chalons or montée Lambert up Colline St-Eutrope (St Eutrope Hill; elevation 97m), once the Romans' lookout point. En route, pass ruins of a 12th-century château, once the residence of the princes of Orange.

Arc de Triomphe   HISTORIC SITE
Orange's 1st-century-AD monumental arch, the Arc de Triomphe – 19m high and wide, and 8m thick – stands on the Via Agrippa. Restored in 2009, its brilliant reliefs commemorate Roman victories in 49 BC with carvings of chained, naked Gauls.

Musée d'Art et d'Histoire   MUSEUM
(www.theatre-antique.com; rue Madeleine Roch; entry incl with Théâtre Antique; ⊙ 9.15am-7pm Jun-Aug, to 6pm Apr, May & Sep, shorter hours Oct-Mar) This small museum contains various finds relating to the theatre's history, including plaques and friezes that once formed part of the scenery, a range of amphora, busts, columns and vases, and a room displaying three rare engraved *cadastres* (official surveys) dating from 77 BC.

⚝ Festivals & Events

Les Chorégies d'Orange   PERFORMING ARTS
(www.choregies.asso.fr; ⊙ Jul & Aug) The Théâtre Antique comes alive with all-night concerts, weekend operas and choral performances. Reserve tickets months ahead, and rooms the year before.

Pont Romain, Vaison-la-Romaine

🛌 Sleeping & Eating

Hôtel Saint Jean   HOTEL €
(📞 04 90 51 15 16; www.hotelsaint-jean.com; 1 cours Pourtoules; s/d/tr/q €75/85/105/125; 🅿️❄️📶) An attractive option with bags of Provençal character, half-built into the hillside of the Colline St-Eutrope. Inside, there are checked fabrics and cosy rooms, with windows overlooking a little patio; outside, the building is all yellow stone and pistachio-coloured shutters. A few of the rooms have walls cut straight into the hill.

⭐ Le Mas Julien   B&B €€
(📞04 90 34 99 49; www.mas-julien.com; 704 chemin de St Jean; d €95-125, studio €110-180; 🅿️❄️📶🐕) Out in the countryside between Orange and Châteauneuf-du-Pape, this delightful farmhouse is the stuff of Provençal dreams: wisteria-clad façade, gorgeous pool, quiet location and rooms that blend contemporary style with rustic charm. There are four rooms and a self-contained studio. Owner Valère caters dinners on request.

Les Saveurs du Marché   FRENCH €
(📞06 14 44 26 63; 24 place Sylvain; 2-/3-/4-course lunch menu €13/16/24, dinner menu €29; ⏰noon-2pm Tue-Sun, 7-9pm Tue-Sat) As the name suggests, market flavours underpin the menu here, from delicious homemade tapenades to pan-seared red mullet drizzled with olive oil and fragrant pesto. The menu changes regularly – the four-course lunch is a steal – but quality can suffer a bit when it gets over-busy, so arrive early.

À la Maison   BISTRO €
(📞04 90 60 98 83; 4 place des Cordeliers; 2-/3-course menu lunch €12.50/15, dinner €25/32; ⏰noon-2pm & 7-10pm Mon-Sat) For dinner on a warm summer night, 'At Home' has the pick of the settings of any of Orange's restaurants, on a side square next to a tinkling fountain shaded by plane trees. The food is fairly standard bistro fare – mainly steaks, salmon, salads and seafood – but it's a shame about the nasty plastic chairs.

La Grotte d'Auguste   FRENCH €€
(📞04 90 60 22 54; www.restaurant-orange.fr; Théâtre Antique, rue Madeleine Roch; lunch/dinner menu from €16/21; ⏰noon-2pm & 7-10pm Tue-Sat) Old-school French dining is the order of the day at Auguste's Cave – an apt name, as the restaurant is half-built into the rocky hillside. Food-wise, expect hearty, meaty dishes presented with care, but few fireworks.

ℹ️ Information

Tourist Office (📞 04 90 34 70 88; www.otorange.fr; place des Frères Mounet; ⏰9am-6.30pm Mon-Sat, 9am-1pm & 2-6.30pm Sun, closed Sun Oct-Mar) Has lots of brochures and handles hotel bookings, and also sells the Roman Pass.

Vaison-la-Romaine

POP 6036

Tucked between seven hills, Vaison-la-Romaine has long been a traditional exchange centre, and it still has a thriving Tuesday market. The village's rich Roman legacy is obvious – 20th-century buildings rise alongside France's largest archaeological site. A Roman bridge crosses the River Ouvèze, dividing the contemporary town's pedestrianised centre and the spectacular walled, cobbled-street hilltop Cité Médiévale – one of Provence's most magical ancient villages – where the counts of Toulouse built their 12th-century castle. Vaison is a good base for jaunts into the Dentelles de Montmirail or Mont Ventoux, but tourists throng here in summer: reserve ahead.

◉ Sights & Activities

Vaison's position is ideal for village-hopping by bicycle. The tourist office stocks excellent brochures detailing multiple cycling circuits (www.escapado.fr), rated by difficulty, from 26km to 91km.

★ Gallo-Roman Ruins   RUINS

(☑04 90 36 50 48; www.provenceromaine.com; adult/child incl all ancient sites, museum & cathedral €8/4; ☺9.30am-6.30pm Jun-Sep, to 6pm Apr & May, 10am-noon & 2-5.30pm Oct-Mar) The ruined remains of Vasio Vocontiorum, the Roman city that flourished here between the 6th and 2nd centuries BC, fill two central Vaison sites. Two neighbourhoods of this once opulent city, Puymin and La Villasse, lie on either side of the tourist office and av du Général de Gaulle. Admission includes entry to the 12th-century Romanesque cloister at Cathédrale Notre-Dame de Nazareth (p25), a five-minute walk west of La Villasse and a soothing refuge from the summer heat.

In Puymin, see houses of the nobility, mosaics, workers' quarters, a temple and the still-functioning, 6000-seat Théâtre Antique (c AD 20). To make sense of the remains (and collect your audioguide; €3), head for the Musée Archéologique Gallo-Roman, which revives Vaison's Roman past with incredible swag – superb mosaics, carved masks and statues that include a 3rd-century silver bust and marble renderings of Hadrian and wife Sabina.

The Romans shopped at the colonnaded boutiques and bathed at La Villasse, where you'll find Maison au Dauphin, which has splendid marble-lined fish ponds.

★ Cité Médiévale   HISTORIC SITE

Wandering around Vaison-la-Romaine's wonderful medieval quarter, you could be forgiven for thinking you've stepped into a forgotten set from *Monty Python and the Holy Grail*. Ringed by ramparts and accessed via the pretty Pont Romain (Roman Bridge), it's a fascinating place to explore, criss-crossed by cobbled alleyways. Look out for the elaborate carvings around many of the doorways as you climb up towards the 12th-century château and its wrap-around vistas.

⌷ Sleeping

Camping du Théâtre Romain   CAMPGROUND €

(☑04 90 28 78 66; www.camping-theatre.com; chemin de Brusquet; sites per 2 people with tent & car €14.90-25.90; ☺mid-Mar–mid-Nov; ⌂✉) A large, well-run campro|und opposite the Théâtre Antique. It gets lots of sun, and there's a pool.

★ Hôtel Burrhus   HOTEL €

(☑04 90 36 00 11; www.burrhus.com; 1 place de Montfort; d €65-96, apt €140; ⓟ✳⌂) From the outside, this looks like a classic town hotel: shutters, stonework and a prime spot on the town square. But inside, surprises await: the arty owners have littered it with modern art, sculptures, funky furniture and colourful decorative details, although the white-walled rooms themselves sometimes feel stark. On sunny days, take breakfast on the plane-tree-shaded balcony overlooking the square.

L'École Buissonière   B&B €

(☑04 90 28 95 19; www.buissonniere-provence.com; D75, Buisson; s/d/tr/q from €55/68/83/100; ⌂) Five minutes north of Vaison, in the countryside between Buisson and Villedieu, hosts Monique and John have transformed their stone farmhouse into a tastefully decorated three-bedroom B&B, which is big on comfort. Breakfast features homemade jam, and there's an outdoor summer kitchen.

Hostellerie Le Beffroi   HISTORIC HOTEL €€

(☑04 90 36 04 71; www.le-beffroi.com; rue de l'Évêché; d €105-195, tr €205-230; ☺Apr-Jan; ⌂✉)

This hotel on the narrow streets of the old town wins hands-down for atmosphere, but you might not feel so enthusiastic once you've lugged your luggage up from the car park. Still, it's awash with history: the two buildings date from 1554 and 1690, and rooms feel appropriately old-fashioned. There's a delightful rose garden and (rather improbably) even a pool.

✕ Eating

Brasseries on place de Montfort vary in quality; restaurants on cours Taulignan are generally better. Dining in Cité Médiévale is limited and pricey.

Maison Lesage   BAKERY €
(2 rue de la République; sandwiches €4-6; ⊙ 7am-1pm & 3-5pm Mon, Tue & Thu-Sat, 7am-1pm Sun) For picnics by the river, this excellent bakery has no shortage of foodie fare: big baguettes, homemade pastries and nougat, and the house speciality, bun-sized meringues in a rainbow of flavours.

★ Bistro du'O   BISTRO €€
(⌨ 04 90 41 72 90; www.bistroduo.fr; rue du Château; lunch/dinner menus from €26/38; ⊙ noon-2pm & 7.30-10pm Tue-Sat) For fine dining in Vaison, this is everyone's tip. The setting is full of atmosphere, in a vaulted cellar in the medieval city (once the château stables), and the chef Philippe Zemour takes his cue from Provençal flavours and daily market ingredients. Top-class food, top setting, tops all round.

Le Moulin à Huile   GASTRONOMY €€€
(⌨ 04 90 36 20 67; www.lemoulinahuile84.fr; quai Maréchal Foch, rte de Malaucène; 2-/3-/4-course menus €29/38/45; ⊙ noon-1.30pm & 7.15-9.30pm Mon, Tue, Fri & Sat, 7.15-9.30pm Thu, noon-1.30pm Sun) This renowned restaurant is still a destination address in Vaison, if only for its lovely riverside setting in a former olive-oil mill. The menus are affordable, and stocked with lots of locally sourced goodies, such as river trout, wood pigeon, and lamb and pork from local farms.

ⓘ Information

Tourist Office (⌨ 04 90 36 02 11; www.vaison-ventoux-tourisme.com; place du Chanoine Sautel; ⊙ 9.30am-noon & 2-5.45pm Mon-Sat year-round, plus 9.30am-noon Sun mid-Mar–mid-Oct, longer hours in summer)

Mont Ventoux & Around

Visible for miles around, Mont Ventoux (1912m) stands like a sentinel over northern Provence. From its summit, accessible by road between May and October, vistas extend to the Alps and, on a clear day, the Camargue.

Because of the mountain's dimensions, every European climate type is represented here, from Mediterranean on its lower southern reaches to Arctic on its exposed northern ridge. As you climb, temperatures can plummet by 20°C, and the fierce mistral wind blows 130 days a year, sometimes at speeds of 250km/h. Bring warm clothes and rain gear, even in summer. You can ascend by road year-round, but you cannot traverse the summit from 15 November to 15 April.

The mountain's diverse fauna and flora have earned the mountain Unesco Biosphere Reserve status. Some species live nowhere else, including the rare snake eagle.

Three gateways – Bédoin, Malaucène and Sault – provide services in summer, but they're far apart.

Biking

Tourist offices distribute *Les Itinéraires Ventoux,* a free map detailing 11 itineraries – graded easy to difficult – and highlighting artisanal farms en route. For more cycling trails, see www.lemontventoux.net. Most cycle-hire outfits also offer electric bikes.

Ventoux Bike Park   CYCLING
(⌨ 04 90 61 84 55; www.facebook.com/ventoux bikepark; Chalet Reynard; half/full day €10/14; ⊙ 10am-5pm Sat & Sun, hours vary Mon-Fri) Near the Mont Ventoux summit, at Chalet Reynard, mountain bikers ascend via rope tow (minimum age 10 years), then descend ramps and jumps down three trails (5km in total). In winter it's possible to mountain bike on snow. Bring a bike, helmet and gloves or rent all gear at Chalet Reynard. Call to check opening times, which are highly weather dependent.

Hiking

The GR4 crosses the Dentelles de Montmirail before scaling Mont Ventoux' northern face, where it meets the GR9. Both traverse the ridge. The GR4 branches eastwards to Gorges du Verdon; the GR9 crosses the Vaucluse Mountains to the Luberon. The essential map for the area is *3140ET Mont Ventoux,* by IGN (www.ign.fr). Bédoin's tourist office stocks maps and brochures detailing walks for all levels.

In July and August tourist offices in Bédoin and Malaucène facilitate night-time expeditions up the mountain to see the sunrise (participants must be over 15 years old).

Les Ânes des Abeilles TOURS
(☑ 04 90 64 01 52; http://abeilles.ane-et-rando.com; rte de la Gabelle, Col des Abeilles; day/weekend from €50/95) A novel means of exploring the Gorges de la Nesque, a spectacular limestone canyon, or nearby Mont Ventoux, is alongside a donkey from Les Ânes des Abeilles. Beasts carry up to 40kg (ie small children or bags).

ⓘ Information

Bédoin Tourist Office (☑ 04 90 65 63 95; www.bedoin.org; Espace Marie-Louis Gravier, 1 rte de Malaucène; ⊙ 9.30am-12.30pm & 2-6pm Mon-Fri, 9.30am-12.30pm & 3-6pm Sat, 10am-12.30pm Sun mid-Apr–mid-Oct, reduced hours mid-Oct–mid-Apr) Excellent source of information on all regional activities; also helps with lodging.

Malaucène Tourist Office (☑ 04 90 65 22 59; http://villagemalaucene.free.fr; place de la Mairie; ⊙ 9.15am-12.15pm & 2.30-5.30pm Mon-Fri, 9am-noon Sat) Small village office with info on Mont Ventoux, but otherwise rather limited on other areas.

Sault Tourist Office (☑ 04 90 64 01 21; www.ventoux-sud.com; av de la Promenade; ⊙ 9.30am-12.30pm & 1.30-6.30pm Mon-Fri, 10am-12.30pm & 2-6.30pm Sat & Sun Jun-Aug, 9am-12.30pm & 2.30-5pm or 6pm Mon-Sat Sep-Mar) Good resource for Mont Ventoux information.

THE LUBERON

Named after the mountain range running east–west between Cavaillon and Manosque, the Luberon is a Provençal patchwork of hilltop villages, vineyards, ancient abbeys and mile after mile of fragrant lavender fields. It's a rural, traditional region that still makes time for the good things in life – particularly fine food and even finer wine. Nearly every village hosts its own weekly market, packed with stalls selling local specialities, especially olive oil, honey and lavender.

Covering some 600 sq km, the Luberon massif itself is divided into three areas: the craggy Petit Luberon in the west, the higher Grand Luberon mountains, and the smaller hills of the Luberon Oriental in the east.

They're all worth exploring, but whatever you do, don't rush – part of the fun of exploring here is getting lost on the back lanes, stopping for lunch at a quiet village cafe, and taking as much time as you possibly can to soak up the scenery.

Apt

POP 11,500 / ELEV 250M

The Luberon's principal town, Apt is edged on three sides by sharply rising plateaux surrounding a river that runs through town. Its Saturday-morning market is full of local colour (and produce), but otherwise Apt is a place you pass through to get somewhere else. Nonetheless, it makes a decent base, if only for a night or two.

Apt is known throughout France for its *fruits confits* (candied fruits, sometimes also known as glacé or crystallised fruit). Strictly speaking, they're not sweets: they're made with real fruit, from which the water is removed and replaced with a sugar syrup to preserve them. As a result, they still look (and more importantly taste) like pieces of the original fruit. There are several makers around town where you can try and buy.

It's also a hub for the 1650-sq-km *Parc Naturel Régional du Luberon* (www.parcdu luberon.fr), a regional nature park crisscrossed by hiking trails.

⊙ Sights & Activities

Musée d'Apt MUSEUM
(Industrial History Museum; ☑ 04 90 74 95 30; 14 place du Postel; adult/child €5/free; ⊙ 10am-noon & 2-6.30pm Mon-Sat Jun-Sep, to 5.30pm Tue-Sat Oct-May) Apt's various industries – ochre-mining, *fruits confits* and faiences (glazed ceramics) – are explored at this modest but well-curated museum in the middle of town. Exhibits include a reconstructed potter's workshop.

Confiserie Kerry Aptunion TOURS
(☑ 04 90 76 31 43; www.lesfleurons-apt.com; D900, Quartier Salignan; ⊙ shop 9am-12.15pm & 1.30-6pm Mon-Sat, 9am-6pm Jul & Aug) Allegedly the largest *fruits confits* maker in the world, this factory 2.5km outside of Apt produces sweets under the prestigious Les Fleurons d'Apt brand. Free tastings are offered in the shop, and you can watch the process in action on guided factory tours; they run at 2.30pm Monday to Friday in July

and August, with an extra tour at 10.30am in August. The rest of the year there's just one weekly tour, usually on Wednesday at 2.30pm; confirm ahead.

- - - - - - - - - - - - - - - - - - -

🛏 Sleeping & Eating

Hôtel le Palais   HOTEL €
(☑ 04 90 04 89 32; www.hotel-restaurant-apt.fr; 24bis place Gabriel-Péri; s/d/tr/q €55/67/80/90; 🛜) Don't go expecting many luxuries at this bargain-basement hotel above a pizza restaurant – but if price is more important than frills, it's a decent option. Rooms are small and very plain, but you're right in the middle of town, and breakfast is a bargain at €6.

★ Le Couvent   B&B €€
(☑ 04 90 04 55 36; www.loucouvent.com; 36 rue Louis Rousset; d €99-140; ☯🛜🅿) Hidden behind a wall in the old town, this enormous *maison d'hôte* occupies a 17th-century former convent. Staying here is as much architectural experience as accommodation: soaring ceilings, stonework, and a grand staircase, plus palatial rooms (one has a sink made from a baptismal font). There's a sweet garden with a little pool, and breakfast is served in the old convent refectory.

Grand Marché d'Apt   MARKET €
(☯ Sat) Apt's huge Saturday-morning market attracts hordes of locals and tourists alike. If you really want to see what a *marché* Provençal is all about, then make it a date in your diary.

There is also a farmers' market every Tuesday morning.

L'Intramuros   FRENCH €€
(☑ 04 90 06 18 87; 120-124 rue de la République; mains €17-19.50; ☯ noon-2pm & 7-9pm Mon-Sat) What fun this place is: an offbeat French restaurant that's stocked to the gunwales with the owners' bric-a-brac finds, from vintage movie posters, antique shop signs and old radios to a collection of sardine cans. It's run by a father-and-son team, and food is filling – expect things like rabbit, duck breast and lamb, plus a choice of pastas.

ⓘ Information

Tourist Office (☑ 04 90 74 03 18; www.luberon-apt.fr; 788 av Victor Hugo; ☯ 9.30am-12.30pm & 2-6pm Mon-Sat, also 9.30am-12.30pm Sun Jul & Aug) Now located in Apt's former train station, the town's tourist office is an excellent source of information for activities, excursions, bike rides and walks.

Maison du Parc du Luberon (☑ 04 90 04 42 00; www.parcduluberon.fr; 60 place Jean Jaurès; ☯ 8.30am-noon & 1.30-6pm Mon-Fri, 9am-noon Sat Apr-Sep, shorter hours Oct-Mar) A central information source for the Parc Naturel Régional du Luberon, with maps, walking guides and general info. There's also a small fossil museum.

North of Apt

Gordes & Around

Arguably the scenic queen of the Luberon's hilltop villages, the tiered village of Gordes seems to teeter improbably on the edge of the sheer rock faces of the Vaucluse plateau from which it rises. A jumble of terracotta

LUBERON BY PEDAL POWER

Don't be put off by the hills – the Luberon is a fantastic destination for cyclists. Several bike routes criss-cross the countryside, including Les Ocres à Vélo, a 51km route that takes in the ochre villages of Apt, Gargas, Rustrel, Roussillon and Villars, and the Véloroute du Calavon, a purpose-built bike path that follows the route of a disused railway line for 28km between Beaumettes in the west (near Coustellet), via Apt, to La Paraire in the west (near St-Martin-de-Castillon). Plans are under way to extend the trail all the way from Cavaillon to the foothills of the Alps, but it'll be a while before it's completed.

For longer trips, Le Luberon à Vélo (☑ 04 90 76 48 05; www.leluberonavelo.com) has mapped a 236km itinerary that takes in pretty much the whole Luberon. Tourist offices stock detailed route leaflets and can provide information on bike rental, luggage transport, accommodation and so on.

Several companies offer e-bikes, which have an electric motor. They're not scooters – you still have to pedal – but the motor helps on the ascents.

rooftops, church towers and winding lanes, it's a living postcard – but unfortunately it's also seethingly popular in summer, so arrive early or late to avoid the worst crowds. Better still, stay for sunset when the village looks at its most beautiful as its honey-coloured stone glows like molten gold.

⊙ Sights

★ Abbaye Notre-Dame de Sénanque
CHURCH

(☑04 90 72 05 72; www.abbayedesenanque.com; adult/child €7.50/3.50; ⊙9-11.30am Mon-Sat Apr-Nov, shorter hours Dec-Mar, guided tours by reservation) If you're searching for that classic postcard shot of the medieval abbey surrounded by a sea of purple lavender, look no further. This sublime Cistercian abbey provides one of the most iconic shots of the Luberon, and it's equally popular these days for selfies. The best displays are usually in July and August. You can wander around the grounds on your own from 9.45am to 11am, but at other times (and to visit the abbey's cloistered interior) you must join a guided tour.

Moulin des Bouillons
DISTILLERY

(☑04 90 72 22 11; www.moulindesbouillons.com; rte de St-Pantaléon; adult/child €5/3.50; ⊙10am-noon & 2-6pm Wed-Mon Apr-Oct) Heading 3.5km south from Gordes along rte de St-Pantaléon (D148), you hit this marvellous rural museum: an olive-oil mill with a 10m-long Gallo-Roman press weighing 7 tonnes – reputedly the world's oldest. The adjoining stained-glass museum showcases beautiful translucent mosaics; a joint ticket costs adult/child €7.50/5.50.

Village des Bories
ARCHITECTURE

(☑04 90 72 03 48; adult/child €6/4; ⊙9am-8pm, shorter hours winter) Beehive-shaped *bories* (stone huts) bespeckle Provence, and at the Village des Bories, 4km southwest of Gordes, an entire village of them can be explored. Constructed of slivered limestone, *bories* were built during the Bronze Age, inhabited by shepherds until 1839, then abandoned until their restoration in the 1970s. Visit early in the morning or just before sunset for the best light. Note that the lower car park is for buses; continue to the hilltop car park to avoid hiking uphill in the blazing heat.

Musée de la Lavande
MUSEUM

(☑04 90 76 91 23; www.museedelalavande.com; D2; adult/child €6.80/free; ⊙9am-7pm May-Sep, 9am-noon & 2-6pm Oct-Apr) To get to grips with Provence's most prestigious crop, this excellent eco-museum makes an ideal first stop. An audioguide and video (in English) explain the lavender harvest, and giant copper stills reveal extraction methods. Afterwards you can take a guided tour of the fields (1pm and 5pm daily May to September). The onsite boutique is an excellent (if pricey) one-stop shop for top-quality lavender products.

There's also a picnic area in the lavender-laden garden. It's located about 7.5km southwest of Gordes on the D2, in the direction of Coustellet.

🛏 Sleeping & Eating

★ Les Balcons du Luberon
B&B €€

(☑06 38 20 42 13; www.lesbalconsduluberon.fr; rte de Murs; d €110-180; 🕸📶) The 'Balconies of the Luberon' is an apt name for this lovely B&B: an 18th-century stone farmhouse with five simple, stylish rooms – the best of which have private patios overlooking epic Luberon scenery. Owner Étienne Marty (a trained chef) offers a sumptuous dinner by reservation (€35).

★ Auberge de Carcarille
HOTEL €€

(☑04 90 72 02 63; www.auberge-carcarille.com; rte d'Apt; d €83-150; P🕸📶🏊) Old outside, new inside: this country hotel marries the atmosphere of a traditional *bastide familiale* (family house) with spotless, modern rooms. There's a delightful garden to wander, and the restaurant serves superior Provençal food (three-course lunch/dinner *menu* €26/44); half-board deals are great value. It's 3km from Gordes, at the bottom of the valley.

Bastide de Gordes
HERITAGE HOTEL €€€

(☑04 90 72 12 12; www.bastide-de-gordes.com; Le Village; r from €290; 🕸📶🏊) Impeccably restored, this deluxe hotel is one of the Luberon's star turns, from the boater-wearing bellboys through to the beamed lobby stuffed with antiques, oil paintings and bookcases. Rooms are enormous and aristocratic (a valley view is essential); spa, gardens, an incredible pool and a trio of restaurants (one Michelin-starred) ice this most indulgent of cakes.

LOCAL KNOWLEDGE: ONCE IN A LIFETIME IN PROVENCE

For a once-in-a-lifetime Provençal experience, look no further than the Domaine de Fontenille (☑ 04 13 98 00 00; www.domainedefontenille.com; rte de Roquefraiche; r from €324; P ⓕ), a glorious hotel 2km northwest of Lauris, at home in an 18th-century mansion framed by sweeping, cypress-filled parkland. Contemporary rooms are elegant; there is a luxurious spa; and then there's Le Champ des Lunes (☑ 04 13 98 00 00; www. domainedefontenille.com; lunch menu €35, dinner €42-108; ⓧ noon-2pm & 7-9.30pm Wed-Sat, noon-2pm Sun).

Overseen by Jérome Faure, who won his first Michelin star at 30, this stellar restaurant is one of the Luberon's most prestigious places to eat. Expect high-class haute cuisine, with impeccably presented dishes dressed with foams, reductions, edible flowers and textural surprises. Lunch is great value – €5 extra buys a glass of wine and coffee.

La Cuisine d'Amelie, the hotel's other restaurant, focuses on simple country flavours and is another lovely spot for lunch (dishes €13 to €18). It's open for lunch and dinner from Friday to Tuesday.

La Boulangerie de Mamie Jane BAKERY €
(☑ 04 90 72 09 34; rue Baptistin Picca; dishes €7-10; ⓧ 6.30am-1pm & 2-6pm Thu-Tue) Those short of time or money in Gordes should follow the locals downhill along rue Baptistin Picca to this pocket-sized *boulangerie* (bakery), which has been in the same family for three generations. Mamie Jane cooks up outstanding bread, pastries, cakes and biscuits, including lavender-perfumed *navettes* (shortbread) and delicious peanut-and-almond brittle known as *écureuil* (from the French for squirrel).

Le Mas Tourteron GASTRONOMY €€€
(☑ 04 90 72 00 16; www.mastourteron.com; chemin de St-Blaise les Imberts; menu lunch/dinner €35/76; ⓧ 12.30-2pm Thu-Sun, 7.30-9.30pm Wed-Sat Apr-Oct) Another one of the Luberon's long-standing tables, overseen by bubbly Elisabeth Bourgeois, it's heavy on Provençal flavours: lots of stuffed aubergines, slow-roasted tomatoes and lashings of olive oil and *herbes de Provence*. The garden setting is lovely, and Elisabeth's husband Philippe handles wine choices. It's 3.5km south of Gordes off the D2.

❶ Information

Tourist Office (☑ 04 90 72 02 75; contact@ luberoncoeurdeprovence.com; place du Château; ⓧ 9am-12.30pm & 1.30-6pm Mon-Sat, from 10am Sun) is inside Gordes' medieval château, which was enlarged and given its defensive Renaissance towers in 1525.

Roussillon

POP 1291

Red by name, red by nature, that's Roussillon – once the centre of local ochre mining, and still unmistakably marked by its crimson colour (villagers are required to paint their houses according to a prescribed palette of some 40 tints). Today it's home to artists' and ceramicists' workshops, and its charms are no secret: arrive early or late.

During WWII the village was the hideout for playwright Samuel Beckett, who helped the local Resistance by hiding explosives at his house and occasionally going on recce missions.

Parking (€3 March to November) is 300m outside the village.

⊙ Sights & Activities

★ **Sentier des Ocres** HIKING
(Ochre Trail; adult/child €2.50/free; ⓧ 9.30am-5.30pm; ⓐ) In Roussillon village, groves of chestnut and pine surround sunset-coloured ochre formations, rising on a clifftop. Two circular trails, taking 30 or 50 minutes to complete, twist through mini-desert landscapes – it's like stepping into a Georgia O'Keeffe painting. Information panels highlight 26 types of flora to spot, the history of local ochre production, and so on. Wear walking shoes and avoid white!

Ôkhra Conservatoire des Ocres et de la Couleur
ARTS CENTRE

(L'Usine d'Ocre Mathieu; ☑ 04 90 05 66 69; www. okhra.com; rte d'Apt; tours adult/student €7/5.50; ⊙ 10am-7pm Jul & Aug, to 6pm Sep-Jun, closed Mon & Tue Jan & Feb; ♿) This art centre is a great place to see ochre in action. Occupying a disused ochre factory on the D104 east of Roussillon, it explores the mineral's properties through hands-on workshops and guided tours of the factory. The shop upstairs stocks paint pigments and other artists' supplies. Bikes can also be rented here.

Mines de Bruoux
HISTORIC SITE

(☑ 04 90 06 22 59; www.minesdebruoux.fr; rte de Croagnes, Gargas; adult/child €8.10/6.50; ⊙ 10am-7pm Jul & Aug, to 6pm Apr-Jun, Sep & Oct) In Gargas, 7km east of Roussillon, this former mine has more than 40km of underground galleries where ochre was once extracted. Around 650m are open to the public, some of which are as much as 15m high. Visits are only by guided tour; reserve ahead as English-language tours are at set times.

🛏 Sleeping & Eating

La Coquillade
FRENCH €€€

(☑ 04 90 74 71 71; www.coquillade.fr; Le Perrotet; menus lunch €42, dinner €75-95; ⊙ 12.30-1.30pm & 7.30-9.30pm mid-Apr–mid-Oct) Overnighting at this luxurious hilltop estate won't suit everyone's budget, but everyone should try to fork out for the great-value bistrot lunch menu. Michelin-starred and run by renowned chef Christophe Renaud, it'll be one of the most memorable meals you'll have in the Luberon. It's a 5km drive south of Roussillon on the D108; look out for signs.

The hotel itself is a stunner, with luxurious rooms (doubles €325 to €390) overlooking a sea of vines.

ⓘ Information

Tourist Office (☑ 04 90 05 60 25; http:// otroussillon.pagesperso-orange.fr; place de la Poste; ⊙ 9am-noon & 1.30-5.30pm Mon-Sat) General information on the village's history and suggestions for walking routes through the surrounding area.

St-Saturnin-lès-Apt

About 9km north of Apt and 10km northeast of Roussillon, St-Saturnin-lès-Apt is refreshingly ungentrified and just beyond the tourist radar. Shops (not boutiques), cafes and bakeries line its cobbled streets. It has marvellous views of the surrounding Vaucluse plateau – climb to the ruins atop the village for knockout views. Or find the photogenic 17th-century windmill, Le Château les Moulins, 1km north, off the D943 towards Sault.

🛏 Sleeping & Eating

Le Saint Hubert
HOTEL €

(☑ 04 90 75 42 02; www.hotel-saint-hubert-luberon. com; rue de la République; d €57-63, tr €73) Charm personified, this quintessential village *auberge* (country inn) on the main street has welcomed travellers since the 18th century and is a gorgeous spot to stay. Rooms are simple but elegant, and the sweeping view of the southern Luberon from valley-facing rooms is breathtaking – especially considering the bargain-basement rates.

The restaurant (two-/three-course lunch menu €16/21, dinner menu €31) is also well worth a visit, with a truly glorious panoramic terrace. If you're staying, ask about half-board.

Le Mas Perréal
B&B €€

(☑ 04 90 75 46 31; www.masperreal.com; Quartier la Fortune; d €140, studios €150; 🅿 ❄) Surrounded by vineyards, lavender fields and cherry orchards, on a vast 7-hectare property outside St-Saturnin-lès-Apt, this farmhouse B&B offers a choice of cosy rooms or self-catering studios, both filled with country antiques and Provençal fabrics. There's a heavenly pool and big garden with mountain views. Elisabeth, a long-time French teacher, offers cooking and French lessons. It's 2km southwest of town along the D2.

L'Estrade
BISTRO €€

(☑ 04 90 71 15 75; 6 av Victor Hugo; mains €14-28; ⊙ noon-2.30pm & 7.30-10.30pm Apr-Oct) Tiny and friendly, this village restaurant is a popular local's tip for solid, fuss-free Provençal cooking. Everything's cooked fresh on the day, so it's worth arriving early to make sure you have the full menu choice.

La Table de Pablo
MODERN FRENCH €€€

(☑ 04 90 75 45 18; www.latabledepablo.com; Les Petits Cléments, Villars; menu €32-45; ⊙ 12.30-2pm & 7.30-9.30pm Mon, Tue, Fri & Sun, 7.30-9.30pm Thu & Sat) Run by top chef Thomas Gallardo, the contemporary feel of this renowned 'semi-gastronomic' restaurant belies its country setting. Funky globe bulbs, downlighters and wooden tables make the dining room look more suited to Paris than Provence – a contrast that's mirrored in the stylish, sophisticated food.

It's 5km east of St-Saturnin on the edge of the village of Villars: look out for the signs for Les-Petits-Cléments.

NORTHEASTERN PROVENCE

Haute-Provence's heady mountain ranges arc across the top of the Côte d'Azur to the Italian border, creating a far-flung crown of snowy peaks and precipitous valleys. To the west, a string of sweet, untouristy hilltop villages and lavender fields drape the Vallée de la Durance. Magical Moustiers Ste-Marie is a gateway to the plunging white waters of Europe's largest canyon, the Gorges du Verdon. In the east, the Vallée des Merveilles wows with 36,000 Bronze Age rock carvings. In the far north are the winter ski slopes and summer mountain retreats of the Ubaye and Blanche Valleys. Outside of ski areas, many establishments close in winter.

Pays de Forcalquier

An oft-overlooked area between the Luberon valley and the Alpine foothills, the Pays de Forcalquier is well off the main tourist radar, meaning that its hilltop villages and rolling farms are usually relatively tranquil even in high summer.

It's the portal to Haute-Provence from the Luberon, and the fastest way in from Marseille too. At its heart lies namesake Forcalquier, famous for its market and absinthe. Saffron grows here, as well as swathes of lavender.

Beyond mass-tourism's radar, Pays de Forcalquier's expansive landscapes comprise wildflower-tinged countryside and isolated hilltop villages. At its heart atop a rocky perch sits its namesake, Forcalquier, a sleepy town that bursts into life once a week during its Monday-morning market. Steep steps lead to the gold-topped citadel and octagonal chapel atop the town.

Some 4km south of Forcalquier, outside the walled city of Mane, is perhaps Provence's

most peaceful address: the 13th-century Prieuré de Salagon (🖉 04 92 75 70 50; www. musee-de-salagon.com; adult/child €8/6; ⊙ 10am-8pm Jun-Aug, to 7pm May & Sep, to 6pm Oct–mid-Dec & Feb-Apr; 🖈) sits amid fields and five themed gardens, including a medieval herb garden, a show garden of world plants, and a wonderfully sweet-smelling Jardin des Senteurs (Garden of Scents) with much native lavender among the mints, mugworts and other fragant plants. Inside the old stone priory, a fascinating permanent exhibition explores lavender and its historical production, uses and culture in Haute-Provence. A stunning repertoire of seasonal concerts and temporary exhibitions – often including great art installations in the chapel – complete the enchanting ensemble.

Forcalquier's quaint pedestrian streets and squares have a generous sprinkling of restaurant terraces. The tourist office (🖉 04 92 75 10 02; www.haute-provence-tourisme.com; 13 place du Bourguet; ⊙ 9am-noon & 2-6pm Mon-Sat) has accommodation information.

Vallée de la Durance

At the western edge of Haute-Provence, the winding waters of the 324km-long Durance River, a tributary of the Rhône, follow the Via Domitia, the road from Italy that allowed the Romans to infiltrate the whole of France. Now it's the autoroute's path, a fast connector between the Alps and the coast.

Come summer, the area's highlight is the Plateau de Valensole, France's lavender capital. Cruise the plateau along the D6 or D8 for arresting views of unfolding purple ripples.

On the other side of the river, Monastère Notre Dame de Ganagobie (🖉 04 92 68 00 04; www.ndganagobie.com; Ganagobie; ⊙ 3-5pm Tue-Sun, shop 10.30am-noon & 2.30-6pm Tue-Sun), a 10th-century Benedictine monastery, is wonderful for a stroll among almond trees, beds of irises and quiet hilltop woods. The 12th-century floor mosaic (depicting dragons) inside the chapel is the largest of its kind in France, and a shop stocks monk-made soaps, honey and music. Ganagobie is signposted off the N96 between Lurs and Peyruis.

French Riviera

With its glistening seas, idyllic beaches and fabulous weather, the Riviera (known as Côte d'Azur to the French) encapsulates many people's idea of the good life.

Although the Riviera does take beach-going very seriously – from nudist beach to secluded cove or exclusive club, there is something for everyone – the beauty is that there is so much more to do than just going to the beach.

Culture vultures will revel in the region's thriving art scene: the Riviera has some fine museums, including world-class modern art, and a rich history to explore in Roman ruins, WWII memorials and excellent museums.

Foodies for their part will rejoice at the prospect of lingering in fruit and veg markets, touring vineyards and feasting on some of France's best cuisines, while outdoor enthusiasts will be spoilt for choice with coastal paths to explore, and snorkelling and swimming galore.

History

The eastern part of France's Mediterranean coast, including the area now known as the Côte d'Azur, was occupied by the Ligurians from the 1st millennium BC. It was colonised around 600 BC by Greeks from Asia Minor, who settled along the coast in the areas of Massalia (present-day Marseille), Hyères, St-Tropez, Antibes and Nice. Called in to help Massalia against the threat of invasion by Celto-Ligurians from Entremont,

the Romans triumphed in 125 BC. They created Provincia Romana – the area between the Alps, the sea and the Rhône River – which ultimately became Provence.

In 1388 Nice, along with the Haute-Provence mountain towns of Barcelonette and Puget-Théniers, was incorporated into the House of Savoy, while the rest of the surrounding Provençal region became part of the French kingdom in 1482. Following an agreement between Napoléon III and the House of Savoy in 1860, the Austrians were ousted and France took possession of Savoy.

Within the Provence–Alpes–Côte d'Azur région, the Côte d'Azur (or Riviera to Anglophones) encompasses most of the départements of the Alpes-Maritimes and the Var. In the 19th century, wealthy tourists flocked here to escape the northern winter, along with celebrated artists and writers, adding to the area's cachet. Little fishing ports morphed into exclusive resorts. Paid holidays for all French workers from 1936 and improved transportation saw visitors arrive in summer, making it a year-round holiday playground. But it's not all play, no work: since the late 20th century, the area inland of Antibes has been home to France's 'Silicon Valley', Sophia Antipolis, the country's largest industrial and technological hub.

Nice

POP 342.522

With its mix of real-city grit, old-world opulence, year-round sunshine, vibrant street life and stunning seaside location, no place in France compares with Nice.

A magnet for sun-seekers and society jet-setters since the 19th century, this bewitching coastal queen has everything going for it – fabulous street markets, an enticing old town, glorious architecture, world-class modern-art museums (thanks to Chagall, Matisse, Picasso and Renoir who fell in love with the place) and a delicious wealth of epicurean restaurants. Nice is far from perfect – it's scruffy in spots, the summertime traffic is horrendous and the beach is made entirely of bum-numbing pebbles – but if you're in town to soak up Riviera vibe, there's no finer spot.

History

Nice was founded around 350 BC by the Greek seafarers who had settled Marseille. They named the colony Nikaia, apparently to commemorate a nearby victory (Nike in Greek). In 154 BC the Greeks were followed by the Romans, who settled further uphill around what is now Cimiez, where there are still Roman ruins.

By the 10th century, Nice was ruled by the counts of Provence but turned to Amadeus VII of the House of Savoy in 1388. In the 18th and 19th centuries it was occupied several times by the French, but didn't definitively become part of France until 1860.

During the Victorian period, the English aristocracy and European royalty enjoyed Nice's mild winter climate. Throughout the 20th century, the city's exceptional art scene spanned every movement from impressionism to new realism. The tram line (customised by artists) and the decision to open all museums for free in 2008 show that art is still very much a part of city life.

- - - - - - - - - - - - - - - - -

◉ Sights

Nice has a number of world-class sights but the star attraction is probably the city itself: atmospheric, beautiful and photogenic, it's a wonderful place to stroll or watch the world go by, so make sure you leave yourself plenty of time to soak it all in.

◉ Vieux Nice

★ **Vieux Nice** CYCLING

(🚊1 to Opéra-Vieille Ville/Cathédrale-Vieille Ville) Getting lost among the dark, narrow, winding alleyways of Nice's old town is a highlight. The layout has barely changed since the 1700s, and it's now packed with delis, restaurants, boutiques and bars, but the centrepiece remains cours Saleya: a massive market square that's permanently thronging in summer. The food market (⊘6am-1.30pm Tue-Sun) is perfect for fresh produce and foodie souvenirs, while the flower market (⊘6am-5.30pm Tue-Sat, 6.30am-1.30pm Sun) is worth visiting just for the colours and fragrances. A flea market (Marché à la Brocante; ⊘7am-6pm Mon) is held on Monday.

Baroque aficionados will adore architectural gems Cathédrale Ste-Réparate (☑04 93 92 01 35; place Rossetti; ⊘ 2-6pm Mon, 9am-noon & 2-6pm Tue-Sun), honouring the city's patron saint; exuberant 16th-century Chapelle de la Miséricorde (☑04 92 00 41 90; cours Saleya; ⊘2.30-5pm Tue Sep-Jun); and 17th-century Palais Lascaris (☑04 93 62 72 40; 15 rue Droite; museum pass 24hr/7 days €10/20, guided visit adult/child €6/free; ⊘10am-6pm Wed-Mon late Jun–mid-Oct, from 11am mid-Oct–late Jun), a frescoed riot of Flemish tapestries, faience (tin-glazed earthenware), gloomy religious paintings and 18th-century pharmacy.

There's also a lively – and very smelly – fish market (⊘6am-1pm Tue-Sun) on place St-François.

★ **Colline du Château** PARK

(Castle Hill; ⊘ 8.30am-8pm Apr-Sep, to 6pm Oct-Mar) FREE For the best views over Nice's red-tiled rooftops, climb the winding staircases up to this wooded outcrop on the eastern edge of the old town. It's been occupied since ancient times; archaeological digs have revealed Celtic and Roman remains, and the site was later occupied by a medieval castle that was razed by Louis XIV in 1706 (only the 16th-century Tour Bellanda remains). There are various entrances, including one beside the tower, or you can cheat and ride the free lift (⊘9am-8pm Jun-Aug, to 7pm Apr, May & Sep, 10am-6pm Oct-Mar).

Port Lympia ARCHITECTURE

(🚊2 to Port Lympia) Nice's Port Lympia, with its beautiful Venetian-coloured buildings, is often overlooked. But a stroll along its quays is lovely, as is the walk to get here: come

Port Lympia

down through Parc du Château or follow quai Rauba Capeu, where a massive war memorial hewn from the rock commemorates the 4000 Niçois who died in both world wars.

👁 Cimiez

Cimiez used to be the playground of European aristocrats wintering on the Riviera. These days, it's Nice's affluent residents who live in the area's beautiful Victorian villas.

★ Musée Matisse   GALLERY
(📞04 93 81 08 08; www.musee-matisse-nice.org; 164 av des Arènes de Cimiez; museum pass 24hr/7 days €10/20; ⊙10am-6pm Wed-Mon late Jun–mid-Oct, from 11am rest of year; 🚌15, 17, 20, 22 to Arènes/Musée Matisse) This museum, 2km north of the city centre in the leafy Cimiez quarter, houses a fascinating assortment of works by Matisse, including oil paintings, drawings, sculptures, tapestries and Matisse's famous paper cut-outs. The permanent collection is displayed in a red-ochre 17th-century Genoese villa in an olive grove. Temporary exhibitions are in the futuristic basement building. Matisse is buried in the Monastère Notre Dame de Cimiez (place du Monastère; ⊙8.30am-12.30pm & 2.30-6.30pm) cemetery, across the park from the museum.

Musée National Marc Chagall   GALLERY
(📞04 93 53 87 20; www.musee-chagall.fr; 4 av Dr Ménard; adult/child €10/8; ⊙10am-6pm Wed-Mon May-Oct, to 5pm Nov-Apr; 🚌15, 22 to Musée Chagall) The strange, dreamlike and often unsettling work of the Belarusian painter Marc Chagall (1887–1985) is displayed at this museum, which owns the largest public collection of the painter's work. The main hall displays 12 huge interpretations (1954–67) of stories from Genesis and Exodus. From the city centre, allow about 20 minutes to walk to the museum (signposted from av de l'Olivetto), or take the bus.

👁 Central Nice

★ Promenade des Anglais   ARCHITECTURE
(🚌8, 52, 62) The most famous stretch of seafront in Nice – if not France – is this vast paved promenade, which gets its name from the English expat patrons who paid for it in 1822. It runs for the whole 4km sweep of the Baie des Anges with a dedicated lane for cyclists and skaters; if you fancy joining them, you can rent skates, scooters and bikes from Roller Station (📞04 93 62 99 05; www.roller-station.fr; 49 quai des États-Unis; skates, boards & scooters per hour/day €5/12, bicycles €5/15; ⊙9am-8pm Jul & Aug, 10am-7pm May, Jun, Sep & Oct, to 6pm Nov-Apr).

A more unusual way to cruise along is an electric Segway from Mobilboard Nice (📞04

91

Nice

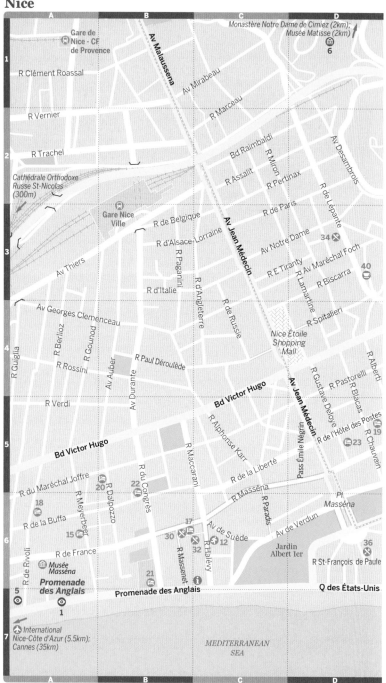

Gare de Nice - CF de Provence

R Clément Roassal

R Vernier

R Trachel

Av Malaussena

Av Mirabeau

R Marceau

Monastère Notre Dame de Cimiez (2km);
Musée Matisse (2km)

6

Bd Raimbaldi

R Assalit

R Miron

R Pertinax

Av Desambrois

R de Lépante

Cathédrale Orthodoxe
Russe St-Nicolas
(300m)

Gare Nice
Ville

R de Belgique

R d'Alsace-Lorraine

R Paganini

R d'Angleterre

R de Paris

Av Jean Médecin

Av Notre Dame

34

R E Tiranty

R Av Maréchal Foch

R Biscarra

R Lamartine

R Spitalieri

40

Av Thiers

Av Georges Clemenceau

R Berlioz

R Gounod

R Rossini

Av Auber

R Paul Déroulède

R d'Italie

R de Russie

Nice Étoile
Shopping
Mall

R Verdi

R Guigla

Av Durante

Bd Victor Hugo

Av Jean Médecin

R Gustave Deloye

R Pastorelli

R Blacas

R Alberti

Bd Victor Hugo

R Alphonse Karr

R Maccarani

R de la Liberté

Pass Émile Negrin

R de l'Hôtel des Postes

R Chauvain

19

23

R du Maréchal Joffre

20

R Dalpozzo

22

R du Congres

R Meyerbeer

18

R de la Buffa

15

R de France

R de Rivoli

Musée
Masséna

Promenade
des Anglais

5

1

International
Nice-Côte d'Azur (5.5km);
Cannes (35km)

17

30

32

R Massenet

R Halévy

12

Av de Suède

R Paradis

R Masséna

Pl
Masséna

Av de Verdun

Jardin
Albert Ier

36

R St-François de Paule

21

Promenade des Anglais

Q des États-Unis

MEDITERRANEAN
SEA

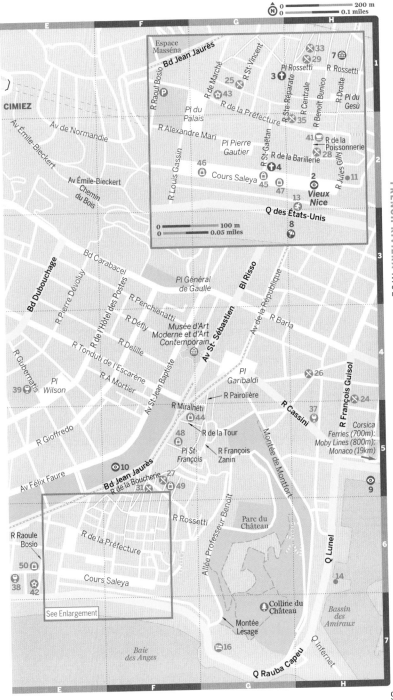

Espace Masséna

Bd Jean Jaurès

R Raoul Bosio

CIMIEZ

Av Émile-Bieckert

Av de Normandie

Av Émile-Bieckert Chemin du Bois

R de Marché

25

43

Pl du Palais

R Alexandre Mari

R de la Préfecture

R Louis Gassin

R St-Vincent

Pl Rossetti

3

Pl Pierre Gautier

R St-Gaëtan

R de la Barillerie

Cours Saleya

46

45

47

4

R Ste-Réparate

R Centrale

R Benoît Bunico

R Rossetti

R Droite

Pl du Gesù

33

29

7

35

41

28

2

Vieux Nice

13

Q des États-Unis

8

R de la Poissonnerie

R Jules Gilly

11

Bd Dubouchage

Bd Carabacel

R Pierre Dévoluy

R de l'Hôtel des Postes

R Penchienatti

R Défly

R Delille

R Tonduti de l'Escarène

R A Mortier

Pl Général de Gaulle

Musée d'Art Moderne et d'Art Contemporain

Av St-Sébastien

Bl Risso

Av de la République

R Barla

Pl Wilson

R Gubernatis

39

R Gioffredo

Av St-Jean Baptiste

R Miralhéti

44

48

Pl St-François

R de la Tour

R François Zanin

Pl Garibaldi

R Pairolière

R Cassini

26

37

R François Guisol

24

Corsica Ferries (700m); Moby Lines (800m); Monaco (19km)

Av Félix Faure

10

Bd Jean Jaurès

R de la Boucherie

31

27

49

R Rossetti

R Raoule Bosio

R de la Préfecture

50

38

42

Cours Saleya

See Enlargement

Baie des Anges

Allée Professeur Benoît

Parc du Château

Montée de Montfort

Q Lunel

9

14

Colline du Château

Montée Lesage

16

Bassin des Amiraux

Q Rauba Capeu

Q Internet

Nice

93 80 21 27; www.mobilboard.com/nice-promenade; 2 rue Halévy, Batiment Ruhl Méridien; 30min/1hr/2hr tour €20/30/50; ⊙9.30am-6pm; ⊒8, 52, 62 to Massenet); the same agency also rents out bikes.

Along the way, keep an eye out for a few of the promenade's landmarks, including the Hôtel Negresco (☑04 93 16 64 00; www. hotel-negresco-nice.com; 37 Promenade des Anglais; ⊒8, 52, 62 to Gambetta/Promenade), the 1929 art-deco Palais de la Méditerranée (☑04 93 27 12 34; www.lepalaisdelamediterranee.com; 13 promenade des Anglais; d €149-879; ✳@☎☒; ⊒8, 52, 62 to Congrès/Promenade) and Niçoise sculptor Sabine Géraudie's giant iron sculpture *La Chaise de SAB* (2014), which pays homage to the city's famous blue-and-white beach chairs.

In 2015 the city of Nice submitted the Promenade des Anglais as a candidate for Unesco World Heritage status – the process can take up to 10 years to complete.

★ **Musée Masséna**   MUSEUM
(☑04 93 91 19 10; 65 rue de France; museum pass 24hr/7 days €10/20; ⊙10am-6pm Wed-Mon late Jun–mid-Oct, from 11am rest of year; ⊒8, 52, 62 to Congrès/Promenade) Originally built as a holiday home for Prince Victor d'Essling (the grandson of one of Napoléon's favourite generals, Maréchal Massena), this lavish belle époque building is another of the city's iconic architectural landmarks. Built between 1898 and 1901 in grand neoclassical style with an Italianate twist, it's now a fascinating museum dedicated to the history of the Riviera – taking in everything from holidaying monarchs to expat Americans, the boom of tourism and the enduring importance of Carnaval.

★ **Musée d'Art Moderne et d'Art Contemporain**   GALLERY
(MAMAC; ☑04 97 13 42 01; www.mamac-nice.org; place Yves Klein; museum pass 24hr/7 days €10/20; ⊙10am-6pm Tue-Sun late Jun–mid-Oct, from 11am

rest of year; 🚇1 to Garibaldi) European and American avant-garde works from the 1950s to the present are the focus of this sprawling multilevel museum. Highlights include many works by Christo and Nice's neorealists: Niki de Saint Phalle, César, Arman and Yves Klein. The building's rooftop also works as an exhibition space (with knockout panoramas of Nice to boot).

Promenade du Paillon
GARDENS

(La Coulée Verte; ⏰7am-9pm Oct-Mar, to 11pm Apr-Sep; 🚇1 to Masséna, Opéra-Vieille Ville or Cathédrale-Vieille Ville) It's hard to imagine that this beautifully landscaped park was once a bus station, a multistorey car park and an ill-loved square. Completed in October 2013, the park unfolds from the Théâtre National to place Masséna with a succession of green spaces, play areas and water features, and is now a favourite among Niçois for afternoon or evening strolls.

Cathédrale Orthodoxe Russe St-Nicolas
CATHEDRAL

(☎09 81 09 53 45; av Nicolas II; ⏰9am-noon & 2-6pm Apr-Oct, 9.30am-noon & 2-5.30pm Nov-Mar; 🚌64, 75 to Tzaréwitch/Gambetta) Built between 1902 and 1912 to provide a big enough church for the growing Russian community, this cathedral, with its colourful onion domes and rich, ornate interior, is the biggest Russian Orthodox church outside Russia. The cathedral boasts dozens of intricate icons – unfortunately, there is very little in the way of explanation for visitors.

✈ Activities & Tours

Nice's beaches are all very pebbly; people with sensitive behinds should therefore opt for a comfy mattress at one of its 14 private beaches (€15 to €25 per day). Out of the free public sections of beach (with lifeguards, first-aid posts and cold showers), Plage Publique des Ponchettes, opposite Vieux Nice, is the most popular (and don't worry about your bottom, many hotels lend you mats!).

Most beaches also offer a raft of activities, from beach volleyball to jet-skis and pedalos.

The best way to discover Nice's rich heritage is to take a guided walking tour. The tourist office (p99) runs a 2½-hour Vieux Nice tour in English (adult/child €12/6), at 9.30am on Saturday.

Centre du Patrimoine
WALKING

(☎04 92 00 41 90; www.nice.fr/fr/culture/patrimoine; 14 rue Jules Gilly; tours adult/child €5/free; ⏰9am-1pm & 2-5pm Mon-Thu, to 3.45pm Fri) The Centre du Patrimoine runs two-hour thematic walking tours. English-language tours must be booked two days in advance. The tourist office has a full listing.

Trans Côte d'Azur
BOATING

(www.trans-cote-azur.com; quai Lunel; ⏰Apr-Oct; 🚇2 to Port Lympia) Trans Côte d'Azur runs one-hour boat cruises along the Baie des Anges and Rade de Villefranche (adult/child €18/13) from April to October. From late May to September it also sails to Île Ste-Marguerite (€40/31, one hour), St-Tropez (€65/51, 2½ hours), Monaco (€38.50/30, 45 minutes) and Cannes (€40/31, one hour).

✳ Festivals & Events

★ Carnaval de Nice
CARNIVAL

(www.nicecarnaval.com; ⏰Feb-Mar) Held over a two-week period in late February and early March since 1294. Highlights include the *batailles de fleurs* (battles of flowers) and the ceremonial burning of the carnival king on Promenade des Anglais, followed by a fireworks display.

Nice Jazz Festival
MUSIC

(www.nicejazzfestival.fr; ⏰Jul) France's original jazz festival has taken on a life of its own, with a jam-packed six-night calendar of performances on two stages in Jardin Albert 1er, and fringe concerts popping up all around town, from Vieux Nice to Massena and the shopping streets around rue de France.

🛏 Sleeping

Accommodation in Nice is excellent and caters to all budgets, unlike many cities on the Côte d'Azur. Hotels charge substantially more during the Monaco Grand Prix. Book well in advance in summer.

★ Hostel Meyerbeer Beach
HOSTEL €

(☎04 93 88 95 65; www.hostelmeyerbeer.com; 15 rue Meyerbeer; dm €25-50, s €80-90, d €90-100; 🚌7, 9, 22, 27, 59, 70 to Rivoli) It's easy to see why this cosy little hostel got voted Best in France in 2018. A welcoming mood prevails throughout, thanks to the congenial, international staff of four, a kitchen small enough to make you feel like you're cooking at home, and a cheerful, immaculate mix of private rooms and four- to eight-bed dorms, each with its own en-suite bathroom.

Villa Saint-Exupéry Beach Hostel
HOSTEL €

(☑ 04 93 16 13 45; www.villahostels.com; 6 rue Sacha Guitry; dm €30-50, d €100; ✱ @ 🛜; 🚊1 to Masséna) Five blocks in from the beach, this long-standing, centrally located city hostel has plenty of pluses: bar, kitchen, gym, sauna, ping-pong, games room and friendly multilingual staff. Dorms sleeping four to 16 all come equipped with private en-suite bathrooms, and there's a host of activities on offer, including yoga, sailing, scuba diving, canyoning and free city walking tours.

Hôtel Solara
HOTEL €

(☑ 04 93 88 09 96; www.hotelsolara.com; 7 rue de France; s €65-75, d €85-115; ⊙ reception 8am-9pm; ✱ 🛜; 🚊 7, 9, 22, 27, 59, 70 to Grimaldi) With a fantastic location on pedestrianised rue de France, small personal fridges for that evening glass of rosé, and sensational terraces on half the rooms, the Solara is pure budget gold. Rooms are small but spotless, and you're right in the heart of the action, a mere block from the beachfront.

Hôtel Wilson
HOTEL €

(☑ 04 93 85 47 79; www.hotel-wilson-nice.com; 39 rue de l'Hôtel des Postes; s €35-57, d €42-82; 🛜; 🚊 7, 9 to Wilson or Pastorelli) Generations of travellers have passed through Jean-Marie's rambling 3rd-floor apartment, where all the rooms have been decorated with potted plants and items collected on his travels in a faintly bohemian, hippie-hangover style (one room's styled after Frida Kahlo, another is stuffed with '70s kitsch, while others have African and Asian flavours). It's faded but winningly friendly and family-run. Cheaper rooms share bathrooms.

★ Hôtel Windsor
BOUTIQUE HOTEL €€

(☑ 04 93 88 59 35; www.hotelwindsornice.com; 11 rue Dalpozzo; d €92-290; ✱ @ 🛜 🛝; 🚊 7, 9, 22, 27, 59, 70 to Grimaldi or Rivoli) Don't be fooled by the staid stone exterior: inside, owner Odile Redolfi has enlisted the collective creativity of several well-known artists to make each of the 57 rooms uniquely appealing. Some are frescoed and others are adorned with experimental chandeliers or photographic murals. The garden and pool out the back are delightful, as are the small bar and attached restaurant.

★ Nice Garden Hôtel
BOUTIQUE HOTEL €€

(☑ 04 93 87 35 62; www.nicegardenhotel.com; 11 rue du Congrès; s €75-85, d €110-140; ⊙ reception 8.30am-9pm; ✱ 🛜; 🚊 7, 9, 22, 27, 59, 70 to Grimaldi) Behind heavy iron gates hides this gem: the nine beautifully appointed rooms – the work of the exquisite Marion – are a subtle blend of old and new and overlook a delightful garden with a glorious orange tree. Amazingly, all this charm and peacefulness is just two blocks from the promenade. Breakfast costs €9.

Hôtel Villa Rivoli
BOUTIQUE HOTEL €€

(☑ 04 93 88 80 25; www.villa-rivoli.com; 10 rue de Rivoli; s €69, d €114-208; ✱ 🛜; 🚊 7, 9, 22, 27, 59, 70 to Rivoli) This charming but strangely shaped villa dates back to 1890, and it's packed with period detail – gilded mirrors, fireplaces, cast-iron balconies and old-world wallpapers, as well as little conifer trees on the balconies and a sweeping marble staircase. Rooms are on the small side, and some are showing their age. There's a small garden and car park beside the hotel.

★ Hôtel La Pérouse
BOUTIQUE HOTEL €€€

(☑ 04 93 62 34 63; www.hotel-la-perouse.com; 11 quai Rauba Capeu; d €247-665; ✱ @ 🛜 🛝) A prime seaside location and boutique hotel style put La Pérouse in a league of its own. Built into the rock cliff-face of Colline du Château, it evokes the spirit of a genteel villa. Lower-floor rooms face a citrus-tree-shaded courtyard and pool; upper-floor rooms have magnificent sea vistas. Smart accent colours and Italian marble bathrooms add flair to the traditional decor.

✕ Eating

Booking is advisable at most restaurants, particularly during the busy summer season. To lunch with locals, grab a pew in the midday sun on one of the many place Garibaldi cafe terraces. There are lots of restaurants on cours Saleya, but quality can be variable, so choose carefully.

★ Mama Baker
BAKERY €

(☑ 06 23 91 33 86; www.facebook.com/mamabakernice; 13 rue de Lépante; items from €2; ⊙ 7am-2pm & 3-7pm Mon-Fri, 7am-6pm Sat; 🚊 4 to Toselli) Great bakeries abound in France, but even here, truly creative artisanal ones stand out. Witness Mama Baker, where organic grains and speciality ingredients go into a host of unique goodies. Don't miss

TOP REGIONAL SPECIALITIES

Nice's eponymous salad (crunchy lettuce, anchovies, olives, green beans and tomatoes in its purest form) has travelled far beyond its original shores. But there is much more to Niçois cuisine than salade Niçoise. Here are five local specialities you should try:

Stockfish Dried cod soaked in running water for a few days and then simmered with onions, tomatoes, garlic, olives and potatoes.

Socca A pancake made of chickpea flour and olive oil cooked on a griddle with sneezing quantities of black pepper.

Daube A rich beef stew of wine, onions, carrots, tomatoes and herbs; the sauce is often served with gnocchi or ravioli.

Petits farcis Stuffed vegetables (generally onions, courgette, courgette flowers, tomatoes and aubergines).

Pissaladière A pizzalike base topped with onions, garlic, olives and anchovies.

Our selection of Niçois restaurants will see you right on stockfish and daube.

the delectable *bouchées aux olives,* soft and crispy bite-sized bits of olive-studded cheesy dough, or *pompe à l'huile,* a semisweet roll flavoured with olive oil and orange blossoms.

★**Chez Palmyre** FRENCH €
(☑ 04 93 85 72 32; 5 rue Droite; 3-course menu €18; ⊙ noon-1.30pm & 7-9.30pm Mon, Tue, Thu & Fri) Look no further for authentic Niçois cooking than this packed, cramped, convivial little space in the heart of the old town. The menu is very meat-heavy, with plenty of tripe, veal, pot-cooked chicken and the like, true to the traditional tastes of Provençal cuisine. It's a bargain, and understandably popular. Book well ahead, even for lunch.

★**La Rossettisserie** FRENCH €
(☑ 04 93 76 18 80; www.larossettisserie.com; 8 rue Mascoïnat; mains €16.50-19.50; ⊙ noon-2pm & 7-10pm Mon-Sat) Roast meat is the order of the day here: make your choice from beef, chicken, veal or lamb, and pair it with a choice of mashed or sautéed potatoes, ratatouille or salad. Simple and sumptuous, with cosy, rustic decor and a delightful vaulted cellar.

Fenocchio ICE CREAM €
(☑ 04 93 80 72 52; www.fenocchio.fr; 2 place Rossetti; 1/2 scoops €2.50/4; ⊙ 9am-midnight Mar-Nov) There's no shortage of ice-cream sellers in the old town, but this *maître glacier* (master ice-cream maker) has been king of the scoops since 1966. The array of flavours is mind-boggling – olive, tomato, fig, beer, lavender and violet to name a few. Dither too long over the 70-plus flavours and you'll never make it to the front of the queue. The

queues at the main branch are long on hot summer days, but they're generally shorter at the second branch (☑ 04 93 62 88 80; 6 rue de la Poissonnerie; 1/2 scoops €2.50/4; ⊙ 9am-midnight Wed-Mon Mar-Nov) around the corner.

Koko Green VEGETARIAN €
(☑ 07 81 63 14 88; www.kokogreen.com; 1 rue de la Loge; weekly specials €15; ⊙ noon-5pm Thu, Fri & Sun, noon-4pm & 7.30-10pm Sat; ☑) At this popular Vieux Nice newcomer, a New Zealander and a naturopath whip up an awesome array of veggie, raw and vegan treats. Weekly specials are globally inspired: Mexican *sopa de tortilla,* Middle Eastern falafel, Vietnamese crêpes – all organic, gluten-free and accompanied by fresh-blended juices. The ultimate showstopper is the vegan cheesecake; dairy-lovers can only marvel at the faux-creaminess!

Badaboom VEGAN €
(☑ 06 71 48 24 01; www.badaboom-nice.net; 11 rue François Guisol; plat du jour €14, with juice €17; ⊙ 8.30am-6pm Mon-Wed, to 10pm Thu & Fri, 10am-5pm Sat; ☑; ☑ 1 to Garibaldi, 2 to Port Lympia) Vegans and vegetarians are in heaven at this little cafe specialising in fresh cold-pressed juices, whole grains, local organic produce and raw desserts. The menu features salads, wraps and daily *plats du jour,* each served with juice for an extra €3.

★**Bar des Oiseaux** FRENCH €€
(☑ 04 93 80 27 33; 5 rue St-Vincent; 3-course lunch menu €20, dinner menus from €30; ⊙ noon-1.45pm & 7.15-9.45pm Tue-Sat) Hidden down a narrow backstreet, this old-town classic has been

97

in business since 1961, serving as a popular nightclub before reincarnating itself as a restaurant (some of its original saucy murals have survived the transition). Nowadays it's a lively bistro serving superb traditional French cuisine spiced up with modern twists. The weekday lunch special offers phenomenal value. Book ahead.

★ La Femme du Boulanger
BISTRO €€

(⏹ 04 89 03 43 03; www.facebook.com/femme duboulanger; 3 rue Raffali; mains €20-25, tartines €16-22; ⏱ 9am-3pm & 7-11pm; ⏹ 8, 52, 62 to Massenet) This back-alley gem with pavement seating is a vision of French bistro bliss. Mains like duck *à l'orange,* honey-balsamic glazed lamb shank, or perfect *steak au poivre* with *gratin dauphinois* (cheesy potatoes) and perfectly tender veggies are followed up with raspberry clafoutis, tiramisu and other scrumptious desserts. Tartines on woodfired homemade bread are the other house speciality.

★ Peixes
SEAFOOD €€

(⏹ 04 93 85 96 15; 4 rue de l'Opéra; small plates €12-19, mains €17-35; ⏱ noon-10pm Tue-Sat) This chic modern seafood eatery is the latest jewel in the crown of Niçois master restaurateur Armand Crespo. All done up in white-and-turquoise nautical decor, with dangling fish eyeball light fixtures and murals of a tentacle-haired mermaid ensnaring a fishing boat, it specialises in fresh local fish turned into delicious ceviches, tartares and Japanese-style tatakis by chefs in the open kitchen.

★ Franchin
FRENCH €€

(⏹ 04 93 87 15 74; www.franchin.fr; 10 rue Massenet; mains €24-31; ⏱ noon-2pm & 7-10pm Wed-Sun; ⏹ 8, 52, 62 to Massenet) White linen tablecloths give this upmarket brasserie an air of formality, but the friendly service dispels any notions of stuffiness, and the food is simply divine. Don't miss the octopus salad with potatoes and chorizo (one of the best appetisers you'll find anywhere on the Côte d'Azur), and ask about the €16 weekday specials (excellent value for money when available).

Olive et Artichaut
PROVENCAL €€

(⏹ 04 89 14 97 51; www.oliveartichaut.com; 6 rue Ste-Réparate; 3-course menu €32, mains €16-28; ⏱ noon-2pm & 7.30-10pm Wed-Sun) There's barely enough room to swing a pan in this tiny street bistro, especially when it's full of diners (as it often is), but it doesn't seem to faze

young Niçois chef Thomas Hubert and his friendly team. He sources as much produce as possible from close-to-home suppliers (Sisteron lamb, Niçoise olives, locally caught fish) and likes to give the old classics his own spin. Wise diners reserve.

Café Paulette
TAPAS €€

(⏹ 04 92 04 74 48; 15 rue Bonaparte; tapas €6-10, mains €11-29; ⏱ 8am-12.30am Wed-Sat; ⏹ 1 to Garibaldi) Chilled and classy Café Paulette has become one of the Petit Marais's favourite hang-outs since opening in 2017. Part cafe, part convivial lunch spot and part evening wine bar, it's especially beloved for its tasty international tapas such as roast squid and barley 'risotto' or Japanese-style sesame-crusted tuna tataki. An ample array of cocktails supplements the solid wine list.

 ## Drinking & Nightlife

Cafe terraces on cours Saleya are lovely for an early-evening aperitif. Vieux Nice's bounty of pubs attracts a noisy, boisterous crowd; most bars have a happy hour from 6pm to 8pm. The trendy area to drink these days is Le Petit Marais in the Port Lympia area, where a clutch of new bars and bistros have opened up.

★ La Part des Anges
WINE BAR

(⏹ 04 93 62 69 80; www.lapartdesanges-nice.com; 17 rue Gubernatis; ⏱ 10am-8.30pm Mon-Thu, to midnight Fri & Sat; ⏹ 7, 9 to Pastorelli or Wilson) The focus of this classy wine shop–bar is organic wines – a few are sold by the glass, but the best selection is available by the bottle, served with homemade tapenades and charcuterie platters. The name means 'the Angel's Share', referring to the alcohol that evaporates as wines age. There are only a few tables, so arrive early or reserve ahead.

★ Beer District
CRAFT BEER

(⏹ 06 75 10 26 36; www.beerdistrict.fr; 13 rue Cassini; ⏱ 6pm-1am Tue-Sat; ⏹ 1 to Garibaldi, 2 to Port Lympia) One of Nice's coolest new nightspots, Beer District pours a regularly rotating line-up of 16 draught microbrews and 50 bottled beers from all over the world. The vibe is chilled and friendly, with free tastes cheerfully offered and little bowls of peanuts for snacking.

★ La Ronronnerie
CAFE

(⏹ 09 51 51 26 50; www.laronronnerie.fr; 4 rue de Lépante; ⏱ 11.30am-6pm Tue-Sat; ⏹ 4 to Sasserno)

Kitties rule the roost at this one-of-a-kind cafe, an absolute must for cat-lovers. Five free-range felines roam about the tables, seeking the right lap to sit in, yawning and stretching on plush pedestals or climbing the tree branch overhead. Meanwhile, humans sip hot beverages and nibble on bagels and cake.

Les Distilleries
Idéales   CAFE
(☑04 93 62 10 66; www.facebook.com/ldinice; 24 rue de la Préfecture; ☺9am-12.30am) The most atmospheric spot for a tipple in the old town, whether you're after one of the many beers on tap or a local wine by the glass. Brick-lined and set out over two floors (with a little balcony perfect for people-watching), it's packed until late. Happy hour is from 6pm to 8pm.

El Merkado   BAR
(☑04 93 62 30 88; www.el-merkado.com; 12 rue St-François de Paule; ☺11am-1.30am Oct-Apr, 10am-2.30am May-Sep) Footsteps from cours Saleya, this hip tapas bar (strapline: 'In Sangria We Trust') struts its vintage stuff on the ground floor of a quintessential Niçois town house. Lounging on its pavement terrace or a sofa with an after-beach cocktail is the thing to do here.

☆ Entertainment

Opéra de Nice   OPERA
(☑04 92 17 40 79; www.opera-nice.org; 4-6 rue St-François de Paule) The vintage 1885 grande dame hosts opera, ballet and orchestral concerts.

Wayne's   LIVE MUSIC
(☑04 93 13 46 99; www.waynes.fr; 15 rue de la Préfecture; ☺10am-2am) One of a strip of raucous drinking holes on the edge of the old town, Wayne's is a proper pub, through and through: plenty of beers on tap, a nightly roster of bands and big-screen sports action. Scruffy as it comes, but great fun if that's what you're in the mood for.

☆ Shopping
Shops abound in Nice, ranging from the boutiques of Vieux Nice and the New Town's designer fashion temples to the enormous Nice Étoile shopping mall. For vintage fashion and contemporary art, meander the hip Petit Marais near place Garibaldi. For gourmet gifts to take home, head for Vieux Nice, where you'll find olive oil, wine, candied fruits and much more.

★ Maison Auer   FOOD
(☑04 93 85 77 98; www.maison-auer.com; 7 rue St-François de Paule; ☺9am-6pm Tue-Sat) With its gilded counters and mirrors, this opulent shop – run by the same family for five generations – looks more like a 19th-century boutique than a sweets shop, but this is where discerning Niçois have been buying their *fruits confits* (crystallised fruit) and *amandes chocolatées* (chocolate-covered almonds) since 1820.

Cave de la Tour   WINE
(☑04 93 80 03 31; www.cavedelatour.com; 3 rue de la Tour; ☺7am-8pm Tue-Sat, to 12.30pm Sun) Since 1947, locals have been trusting the owners of this atmospheric *cave* (wine cellar) to find the best wines from across the Alpes-Maritimes and Var. It's a ramshackle kind of place, with upturned wine barrels and blackboard signs, and a loyal clientele, including market traders and fishmongers getting their early-morning wine fix. Lots of wines are available by the glass.

Friperie Caprice   VINTAGE
(☑09 83 48 05 43; www.facebook.com/caprice vintageshop; 12 rue Droite; ☺2-7pm Mon, 11am-1.30pm & 2.30-7pm Tue-Sat) Nice's favourite vintage shop is a treasure trove of clothing, jewellery and accessories spanning much of the 20th century; what really sets it apart is the generous advice and assistance of amiable owner Madame Caprice, who knows every piece in the shop.

ⓘ Information
Tourist Office (☑04 92 14 46 14; www.nicetourisme.com; 5 Promenade des Anglais; ☺9am-7pm daily Jun-Sep, to 6pm Mon-Sat Oct-May; 🖥; 🚌8, 52, 62 to Massenet) Nice's main tourist office on Promenade des Anglais provides a wealth of resources, including maps, brochures, information about attractions and help booking accommodation.

ⓘ Getting There & Away

AIR
Nice-Côte d'Azur Airport (NCE; ☑08 20 42 33 33; www.nice.aeroport.fr; 🖥; 🚌98, 99, 🚌2) is France's second-largest airport and has international flights to Europe, North Africa and the USA, with regular and low-cost airlines. The airport has two terminals, linked by a free shuttle bus.

BOAT

Corsica Ferries (📞 04 92 00 42 76; www.
corsicaferries.com; quai du Commerce; 🚌 2 to
Port Lympia) and **Moby Lines** (📞 08 00 90 11
44; www.mobylines.fr; Quai du Commerce; 🚌 2
to Port Lympia) offer regular ferry services from
Nice to Corsica. Corsica Ferries also serves
Golfo Aranci in Sardinia.

ℹ️ Getting Around

BICYCLE

Vélo Bleu (📞 04 93 72 06 06; www.velobleu.org)
is Nice's shared-bicycle service. It's great value
and very convenient for getting round town,
with 100-plus stations around the city – pick up
your bike at one, return it at another.

One-day/weeklong subscriptions cost
€1.50/5, plus usage: free for the first 30 minutes, €1 for the next 30, then €2 per hour there-
after. Some stations are equipped with terminals
to register directly with a credit card; otherwise
you'll need a mobile phone.

The handy Vélo Bleu app allows you to find
your nearest station, gives real-time information
about the number of bikes available at each and
calculates itineraries.

CAR & MOTORCYCLE

Traffic, a confusing one-way system, and pricey
parking mean driving in Nice is a bad idea – it's
better to explore the city first, then head back
out to the airport and rent your car for onward
travel there.

Holiday Bikes (📞 04 93 16 01 62; www.loca
-bike.fr; 34 av Auber; 24hr rental 50cc/125cc
scooter from €32/57; ⏰ 9.30am-12.30pm & 2.30-
6.30pm Mon-Sat year-round, plus 10am-noon
& 5-6.30pm Sun Jun-Aug; 🚌 1 to Gare Thiers)
rents out scooters and motorcycles. It has **another office** (📞 04 93 04 15 36; 6 rue Massenet;
⏰ 9.30am-12.30pm & 2.30-6.30pm Mon-Sat year-
round, plus 10am-noon & 5-6.30pm Sun Jun-Aug;
🚌 8, 52, 62 to Massenet) just off the Promenade
des Anglais.

St-Paul de Vence

POP 3451

Once upon a time, St-Paul de Vence was a
small medieval village atop a hill looking
out to sea. Then came the likes of Chagall
and Picasso in the postwar years, followed
by showbiz stars such as Yves Montand and
Roger Moore, and this once quiet town shot
to fame. The village is now home to dozens
of art galleries as well as the renowned Fondation Maeght.

St-Paul's tiny cobbled lanes get over-
whelmingly crowded in high season – come
early or late to beat the rush.

👁 Sights & Activities

Across from the entrance to the fortified village, the *pétanque* pitch, where many a film
star has had a spin, is the hub of village life.
The tourist office rents out balls (€2) and organises one-hour *pétanque* lessons (€5 per
person; reserve in advance).

Strolling the narrow streets is how most
visitors pass time in St-Paul de Vence. The
village has been beautifully preserved and
the panoramas from the ramparts are stunning. The main artery, rue Grande, is lined
with art galleries. The highest point in the
village is occupied by the Église Collégiale;
the adjoining Chapelle des Pénitents Blancs
was redecorated by Belgian artist Folon.

Many more artists lived or passed
through St-Paul de Vence at various times,
among them Soutine, Léger, Cocteau, Matisse and Chagall. The latter is buried with
his wife Vava in the cemetery at the village's
southern end (immediately to the right as
you enter). The tourist office runs a series
of informative, themed, 90-minute guided
tours (adult/child €5/free).

Fondation Maeght   MUSEUM
(📞 04 93 32 81 63; www.fondation-maeght.com; 623
chemin des Gardettes; adult/child €15/10; ⏰ 10am-
7pm Jul-Sep, to 6pm Oct-Jun) St-Paul's renowned
art museum features works by a who's who
of 20th-century artists – including many
who found inspiration along the Côte d'Azur. From pieces by Georges Braque, Vassily
Kandinsky and Marc Chagall to spooky
sculptures by Alberto Giacometti and glass-
works by Joan Miró, it's a treasure trove of
great art – although works from the permanent collection are often disappointingly
confined to a single room to make room
for temporary exhibits (which are usually
excellent, and well worth checking out).
Find the fondation 500m downhill from
the village.

The building was designed by Josep
Lluís Sert and is a masterpiece in itself, in-
tegrating the works of the very best: a Giacometti courtyard, Miró sculptures dotted
across the terraced gardens, coloured-glass
windows by Braque and mosaics by Chagall
and Tal-Coat.

🛏 Sleeping & Eating

Villa St Paul   B&B €€
(📞04 93 72 58 71; www.villasaintpauldevence.com;
293 Chemin Fontmurado; r €78-150, apt €98-240;
🛜🌊) At this attractive oasis 1km below St-
Paul, friendly young hosts David and Jean-
nette welcome guests with three spacious,
comfortable rooms and a grassy pool area
for lounging. Days begin with abundant
breakfasts featuring fresh-squeezed orange
juice, croissants, a variety of cheeses and
eggs cooked to order. The pricier adjoining
Étoile de St-Paul features six more rooms
and its own *hammam*.

★ Les Cabanes d'Orion   B&B €€€
(📞06 75 45 18 64; www.orionbb.com; Impasse des
Peupliers, 2436 chemin du Malvan; d €230-285;
🛜🌊) Dragonflies flit above water lilies in
the natural swimming pool, while guests
slumber amid a chorus of frogs and cicadas
in luxurious cedar-wood tree houses at this
enchanting, ecofriendly B&B. Children are
well catered for with mini-*cabanes* in two of
the tree houses. There's a minimum two- to
four-night stay from May to September.

La Colombe d'Or   HOTEL €€€
(📞04 93 32 80 02; www.la-colombe-dor.com; place
de Gaulle; d €250-430; ❄🛜🌊) This world-
famous inn could double as the Fondation
Maeght's annexe: the 'Golden Dove' was
party HQ for dozens of 20th-century artists
(Chagall, Braque, Matisse, Picasso etc) who
paid for their meals in kind, resulting in an
extraordinary private art collection. Rooms
are strung with unique pieces, as are the
restaurant (mains €29-49; ⊙noon-2.30pm & 7.30-
10.30pm late Dec-Oct) and garden.

★ Le Tilleul   MODERN FRENCH €€
(📞04 93 32 80 36; www.restaurant-letilleul.com;
place du Tilleul; menus €25-29, mains €15-32;
⊙8.30am-10.30pm; 🖋) Considering its location on the *remparts,* this place could
have easily plumbed the depths of a typical
tourist trap. But it hasn't. Instead, divine
and beautifully presented dishes grace your
table, complemented by an all-French wine
list and blissful terrace seating under the
shade of a big lime-blossom tree. Open for
breakfast and afternoon tea too.

ⓘ Information

Tourist Office (📞04 93 32 86 95; www.saint
-pauldevence.com; 2 rue Grande; ⊙10am-7pm
Jun-Sep, to 6pm Oct-May, closed 1-2pm Sat

& Sun) Runs a series of informative, themed
guided tours that delve into the village's
illustrious past. Some tours are also available in
English. Book ahead. Also organises *pétanque*
lessons.

Vence
POP 18,393

Some visitors only come to Vence to see Matisse's otherworldly Chapelle du Rosaire at
the edge of town. Yet Vence deserves more
than a flying visit. It's well worth lingering a while to explore the city's charming
and well-preserved medieval centre, much
of which dates back to the 13th century.
Sample some of Vence's gastronomic talent on restaurant-fringed place du Peyra,
stroll through lovely place du Frêne with
its 500-year-old ash tree, or take time to ap-
preciate the Marc Chagall mosaic in Vieux
Vence's cathedral. A fruit-and-veg market
fills place du Jardin several mornings a
week, with antiques on Wednesday.

◉ Sights

Much of the historical centre dates back
to the 13th century. The Romanesque
cathedral on the eastern side of the square
was built in the 11th century on the site of
an old Roman temple. It contains Chagall's
mosaic of Moses (1979), appropriately
watching over the baptismal font.

★ Chapelle du Rosaire   ARCHITECTURE
(Rosary Chapel; 📞04 93 58 03 26; www.vence.fr/
the-rosaire-chapel; 466 av Henri Matisse; adult/child
€7/4; ⊙10am-noon & 2-6pm Tue, Thu & Fri, 2-6pm
Wed & Sat Apr-Oct, to 5pm Nov-Mar) An ailing
Henri Matisse moved to Vence in 1943 to
be cared for by his former nurse and mod-
el, Monique Bourgeois, who'd since become
a Dominican nun. She persuaded him to
design this extraordinary chapel for her
community. The artist designed everything
from the decor to the altar and the priests'
vestments. From the road, you can see the
blue-and-white ceramic roof tiles, wrought-
iron cross and bell tower. Inside, light floods
through the glorious blue, green and yellow
stained-glass windows.

The colours respectively symbolise
water/the sky, plants/life, the sun/God's
presence; the western windows display Matisse's famous seaweed motif, those on the
southern side a stylised, geometric leaf-like
shape.

Marché Provençal

A line image of the Virgin Mary and child is painted on white ceramic tiles on the northern interior wall. The eastern wall is dominated by the bolder Chemin de Croix (Stations of the Cross). St Dominic overlooks the altar. Matisse also designed the chapel's stone altar, candlesticks and cross. The beautiful priests' vestments are displayed in a separate hall upstairs.

🛏 Sleeping & Eating

Le 2   B&B €€
(☑06 15 37 22 40, 04 93 24 42 58; www.le2avence.fr; 2 rue des Portiques; d incl breakfast €108-128; ✳🛜)
This 'bed and bistro,' as it's tagged itself, is a welcome addition to staid Vence. Nicolas and his family have turned this medieval townhouse into a hip establishment offering four very modern rooms upstairs and a popular vegetarian restaurant down below. Value and atmosphere guaranteed.

⭐**Restaurant**
La Litote   MODERN FRENCH €€
(☑04 93 24 27 82; www.lalitote-vence.com; 5 rue de l'Évêché; 2-/3-course lunch menus €18/22, dinner menus €29/34; ☺noon-2.30pm & 7-10pm, closed Tue Jun-Sep, closed Sun evening & Mon Oct-May)
In the heart of Vence's old town, La Litote is the very picture of a village bistro, with tables set out on the square and blackboard menus filled with seasonal classics. Expect stews, supremes and steaks in win-ter, grilled fish and salads in summer, and delicious desserts year-round. Homey and lovely.

Antibes & Juan-les-Pins

POP 76,119

With its boat-bedecked port, 16th-century ramparts and narrow cobblestone streets festooned with flowers, lovely Antibes is the quintessential Mediterranean town. Picasso, Max Ernst and Nicolas de Staël were capti-vated by Antibes, as was a restless Graham Greene (1904–91) who settled here with his lover, Yvonne Cloetta, from 1966 until the year before his death.

Greater Antibes embraces Cap d'Antibes, an exclusive green cape studded with luxuri-ous mansions, and the modern beach resort of Juan-les-Pins. The latter is known for its 2km-long sandy beach and nightlife, a leg-acy of the sizzling 1920s when Americans swung into town with their jazz music and oh-so-brief swimsuits.

◎ Sights & Activities

Vieil Antibes   HISTORIC SITE
Ringed by sturdy medieval walls and criss-crossed with lanes and shady squares, old Antibes is a delightful place for a wander. The wonderful Marché Provençal (cours

Masséna; ⊙7am-1pm Tue-Sun Sep-Jun, daily Jul & Aug) is old Antibes' beating heart, sheltered by a 19th-century cast-iron roof and packed with stalls selling olives, cheese, vegetables, tapenades and other Provençal goodies until around 1pm.

Along the edge of the old town, views from the sea walls stretch all the way to Nice (spot the runway) and inland to the snowy Alps. There's one section of the ramparts overlooking place du Verdun where you can walk along and imagine yourself operating a medieval cannon.

Musée Picasso   MUSEUM

(☑04 92 90 54 26; www.antibes-juanlespins.com/culture/musee-picasso; Château Grimaldi, 4 rue des Cordiers; adult/concession €6/3; ⊙10am-6pm Tue-Sun mid-Jun–mid-Sep, 10am-1pm & 2-6pm Tue-Sun rest of year) Picasso himself said, 'If you want to see the Picassos from Antibes, you have to see them in Antibes'. The 14th-century Château Grimaldi was Picasso's studio from July to December 1946 and now houses an excellent collection of his works and fascinating photos of him. The sheer variety – lithographs, paintings, drawings and ceramics – shows how versatile and curious an artist Picasso was. The museum also has a room dedicated to Nicolas de Staël, another painter who adopted Antibes as home.

Fort Carré   MONUMENT

(☑04 92 90 52 13; av 11 Novembre; guided tour adult/child €3/free; ⊙10am-1pm & 2-6pm Tue-Sun Jun-Oct, 10am-12.30pm & 1.30-4.30pm Tue-Sun Nov-May) The impregnable 16th-century Fort Carré, enlarged by Vauban in the 17th century, dominates the approach to Antibes from Nice. It served as a border defence post until 1860, when Nice, until then in Italian hands, became French. Tours depart half-hourly; some guides speak English.

Cap d'Antibes   WALKING

Cap d'Antibes' 4.8km of wooded shores are the perfect setting for a walk-swim-walk-swim afternoon. Paths are well sign-posted and easy to follow. The tourist office maps show itineraries.

 Festivals & Events

Jazz à Juan   MUSIC

(www.jazzajuan.com; Les Jardins du Jazz, bd Baudoin; ⊙mid-Jul) This major festival has been running for more than 50 years. Every jazz great

has performed here, and the festival continues to attract big music names.

🛏 Sleeping

Le Relais du Postillon   HOTEL €€

(☑04 93 34 20 77; www.relaisdupostillon.com; 8 rue Championnet; s from €65, d €85-149; ⊙reception 7.30am-11pm; ❋⑧) This stone-walled former coaching hotel has a great location opposite a small park and square on the edge of the old town. Rooms are rather charming, especially if you bag one at the front, which have their own dinky balconies overlooking the square. The ground-floor cafe is a lovely spot for breakfast, too.

Hôtel La Jabotte   B&B €€

(☑04 93 61 45 89; www.jabotte.com; 13 av Max Maurey; d €154-214, q €254; ❋@⑧) Just 150m inland from Plage de la Salis and 2km south of the old town towards Cap d'Antibes, this pretty little hideaway makes a cosy base. Hot pinks, sunny yellows and soothing mauves dominate the homey, feminine decor, and there's a sweet patio where breakfast is served on sunny days. There's a minimum stay of three nights in summer.

✕ Eating

★L'Atelier Jean-Luc Pelé   SANDWICHES €

(☑04 92 95 78 21; www.jeanlucpele.com; 27 rue de la République; sandwiches from €5; ⊙7am-7pm) This branch of Jean-Luc Pelé's stellar Cannes bakery is a welcome addition to Antibes' lunch line-up. Gourmet bagels, wraps, soups, quiches and sandwiches come in all kinds of creative combos (€7.50 to €11) including a drink and a sinful cake from the patisserie counter. There's also a divine array of chocolates.

La Ferme au Foie Gras   DELI €

(☑04 93 34 26 50; www.vente-foie-gras.net; 35 rue Aubernon; sandwiches €4-9; ⊙8am-7pm Tue-Sun) Just down the hill from the Marché Provençal, this heartwarming deli sells local goodies like charcuterie, cheeses and jams, and makes delicious gourmet sandwiches – with ingredients ranging from foie gras to smoked duck and salmon, mozzarella, camembert and more.

★Nacional   INTERNATIONAL €€

(☑04 93 61 77 30; www.restaurant-nacional-antibes.com; 61 place Nationale; tapas €8-21, mains €21-38; ⊙noon-2pm & 7-10pm Tue-Thu, to 10.30pm Fri & Sat)

'Beef & Wine' is the strapline of this contemporary wine-bar-styled space, so that should give you some idea of the focus here. It's popular for its burgers, steaks in pepper or port sauce, and other grilled meats. The in-crowd adores it for aperitifs and tapas, best sampled on the walled patio garden hidden away at the back.

Drinking & Nightlife

Absinthe Bar   BAR
(☑ 04 93 34 93 00; www.facebook.com/absinthe antibes; 25 cours Masséna; ⊘ 10.30am-7.30pm Tue-Thu, to 12.30am Fri & Sat) Flirt with the green fairy in this convivial cellar, with original 1860 zinc bar, a few round tables and all the accessories (four-tapped water fountain, sugar cubes etc). Live piano music on Friday and Saturday evenings enhances the ambiance.

La Siesta Beach Club   CLUB
(☑ 04 93 33 31 31; www.joa-casino.com; 2000 rte Bord de Mer; ⊘ 6pm-1am Sun-Thu, to 2am Fri & Sat mid-Jun–early Sep) This legendary establishment is famous up and down the coast for its summer beachside nightclub and late-night dancing under the stars. There are DJs nightly, plus live music on Fridays and Saturdays. Find it 4km north of Vieil Antibes on the D6098.

ⓘ Information

Tourist Office (☑ 04 22 10 60 10; www.antibesjuanlespins.com; 42 av Robert Soleau; ⊘ 9am-7pm daily Jul & Aug, 9.30am-12.30pm & 2-5pm Mon-Sat, 9am-1pm Sun Sep-Jun)

Menton

POP 28.231

Last stop on the Côte d'Azur before Italy, the seaside town of Menton offers a glimpse of what the high life on the Riviera must have been like before the developers moved in. With its sunny climate, shady streets and pastel mansions – not to mention a lovely old port – it's one of the most attractive towns on the entire coast. Menton's old town is a cascade of pastel-coloured buildings. Add a fantastic museum dedicated to the great artist and film director Jean Cocteau, as well as several excellent restaurants, and Menton really is a must.

To French people, the town is also known for its lemons, which are renowned for their flavour and celebrated every February with a big lemon-themed party.

⊙ Sights & Activities

The town's epicentre is the bustling, pedestrianised rue St-Michel, with its ice-cream parlours and souvenir shops.

Menton's old town is a cascade of pastel-coloured buildings. Meander the historic quarter all the way to the Cimetière du Vieux Château (montée du Souvenir; ⊘ 7am-8pm Apr-Oct, 8am-5pm Nov-Mar) for great views. From place du Cap a ramp leads to Southern France's grandest baroque church, the Italianate Basilique St-Michel Archange (place de l'Église St-Michel; ⊘ 10am-noon & 4-6pm Mon-Fri Jul & Aug, 10am-noon & 3-5pm Mon-Fri Sep-Jun); its creamy façade is flanked by a 35m-tall clock tower and 53m-tall steeple (1701–03).

★ **Musée Jean Cocteau Collection Séverin Wunderman**   GALLERY
(☑ 04 89 81 52 50; www.museecocteaumenton. fr; 2 quai de Monléon; adult/child Jun-Oct €10/ free, Nov-May €8/free; ⊘ 10am-6pm Wed-Mon) Art collector Séverin Wunderman donated some 1500 Cocteau works to Menton in 2005 on the condition that the town build a dedicated Cocteau museum. And what a museum Menton built: this futuristic, low-rise building is a wonderful space to make sense of Cocteau's eclectic work. Its collection includes drawings, ceramics, paintings and cinematographic work, with exhibits rotating annually. Admission includes Cocteau-designed Musée du Bastion.

Musée du Bastion   GALLERY
(quai Napoléon III; adult/child Jun-Oct €10/free, Nov-May €8/free; ⊘ 10am-6pm Wed-Mon) Cocteau loved Menton. It was following a stroll along the seaside that he got the idea of turning a disued 17th-century bastion (1636) on the seafront into a monument to his work. He restored the building himself, decorating the alcoves, outer walls, reception hall and floors with pebble mosaics. The works on display change regularly. Admission includes entry to the Musée Jean Cocteau.

Jardin de la Serre de la Madone   GARDENS
(☑ 04 93 57 73 90; www.serredelamadone.com; 74 rte de Gorbio; adult/child €8/4; ⊘ 10am-6pm Tue-Sun Apr-Oct, to 5pm Jan-Mar, closed Nov & Dec) Beautiful if slightly unkempt, this garden was designed by American botanist Lawrence Johnston. He planted dozens of rare plants

picked up from his travels around the world. Abandoned for decades, it has been mostly restored to its former glory. Guided tours (1½ hours) take place daily at 3pm. Take Zest (☑ 04 93 35 93 60; www.zestbus.fr; €1.50, 15 minutes) bus 7 from Menton's train or bus station to the Serre de la Madone stop.

🛏 Sleeping & Eating

In the old town, pedestrianised rue du Vieux Collège is worth a meander for its tasty line-up of eateries. Rue St-Michel is littered with touristy shops selling lemon-based products, including limoncello, lemon-ade, lemon-infused olive oil and lemon preserves.

Hôtel Lemon   HOTEL €
(☑ 04 93 28 63 63; www.hotel-lemon.com; 10 rue Albert 1er; s €65, d €73-85; 🛜) Hôtel Lemon sits in an attractive 19th-century villa with a pretty garden, opposite a school. Its spacious minimalist rooms are decked out in shades of white with bright red or lemon-yellow bathrooms. Breakfast costs €9.

⭐ Hôtel Napoléon   BOUTIQUE HOTEL €€
(☑ 04 93 35 89 50; www.napoleon-menton.com; 29 porte de France; d €95-330, junior ste €149-450; ✳ @ 🛜 🌊) Standing tall on the seafront, the Napoléon is Menton's most stylish sleeping option. Everything from the pool to the restaurant-bar and the back garden (a haven of freshness in summer) has been beautifully designed. Rooms are decked out in white and blue, with Cocteau drawings on headboards. Sea-facing rooms have balconies but are a little noisier because of the traffic.

Au Baiser du Mitron   BAKERY €
(The Baker's Kiss; ☑ 04 93 57 67 82; www.aubaiserdumitron.com; 8 rue Piéta; items from €1;

☺ 8am-7pm Tue-Sun) This one-of-a-kind *boulangerie* showcases breads from the Côte d'Azur, inland Provence and other favourite spots from baker-owner Kevin Le Meur's world travels. Everything is baked in a traditional *four à bois* (wood bread oven) from 1906, using 100% natural ingredients and no preservatives. The *tarte au citron de Menton* (Menton lemon tart) is the best there is.

Le Bistrot des Jardins   PROVENCAL €€
(☑ 04 93 28 28 09; www.le-bistrot-des-jardins.fr; 14 av Boyer; 2-/3-course menus lunch €27/33, dinner €33/40; ☺ noon-2pm & 7.30-9.30pm Tue-Sat, noon-2pm Sun) Reservations are required at this delightful patio garden restaurant with tables clothed in lilac languishing al fresco between flowering magnolias and aromatic pots of thyme, sage and other Provençal herbs. The traditional, market-inspired cuisine is equally attractive.

⭐ Le Mirazur   GASTRONOMY €€€
(☑ 04 92 41 86 86; www.mirazur.fr; 30 av Aristide Briand; lunch menus €80-110, dinner menus €110-210; ☺ 12.15-2pm & 7.15-10pm Wed-Sun Mar-Dec) Design, cuisine and sea views (the full sweep of the Med) are all spectacular at this 1930s villa with a twinset of Michelin stars. This is the culinary kingdom of daring Argentinian chef Mauro Colagreco, who flavours dishes not with heavy sauces but with herbs and flowers from Le Mirazur's dazzling herb and flower garden, citrus orchard and vegetable patch.

Find it 3km northeast of Menton off the coastal D6007 to Italy. Cooking classes too.

ℹ Information

Tourist Office (☑ 04 92 41 76 76; www.tourisme-menton.fr; 8 av Boyer; ☺ 9am-7pm Jul & Aug, 9am-12.30pm & 2-6pm Mon-Sat Sep-Jun)

ROAD TRIP ESSENTIALS

France Driving Guide

With stunning landscapes, superb highways and one of the world's most scenic and comprehensive secondary road networks, France is a road-tripper's dream come true.

DRIVING LICENCE & DOCUMENTS

Drivers must carry the following at all times:

➡ passport or an EU national ID card

➡ valid driving licence (*permis de conduire*; most foreign licences can be used in France for up to a year)

➡ car-ownership papers, known as a *carte grise* (grey card)

➡ proof of third-party liability *assurance* (insurance)

An International Driving Permit (IDP) is not required when renting a car but can be useful in the event of an accident or police stop, as it translates and vouches for the authenticity of your home licence.

Road Trip Websites

AUTOMOBILE ASSOCIATIONS

RAC (www.rac.co.uk/driving-abroad/france) Info for British drivers on driving in France.

CONDITIONS & TRAFFIC

Bison Futé (www.bison-fute.equipement.gouv.fr)

Les Sociétés d'Autoroutes (www.autoroutes.fr)

ROUTE MAPPING

Mappy (www.mappy.fr)

Via Michelin (www.viamichelin.com)

Driving Fast Facts

Right or left? Drive on the right

Legal driving age 18

Top speed limit 130km/h on *autoroutes* (highways, motorways)

Signature car Citroën 2CV

INSURANCE

Third-party liability insurance (*assurance au tiers*) is compulsory for all vehicles in France, including cars brought in from abroad. Normally, cars registered and insured in other European countries can circulate freely in France, but it's a good idea to contact your insurance company before you leave home to make sure you have coverage – and to check whom to contact in case of a breakdown or accident.

If you get into a minor accident with no injuries, the easiest way for drivers to sort things out with their insurance companies is to fill out a *Constat Aimable d'Accident Automobile* (European Accident Statement), a standardised way of recording important details about what happened. In rental cars it's usually in the packet of documents in the glove compartment. Make sure the report includes any information that will help you prove that the accident was not your fault. Remember, if it *was* your fault you may be liable for a hefty insurance deductible/excess. Don't sign anything you don't fully understand.

Local Expert: Driving Tips

Driving tips for France from Bert Morris, research consultant for IAM (www.iam.org.uk) and former motoring policy director for the AA:

➡ First thing if you're British: watch your instinct to drive on the left. Once I was leaving a supermarket using the left-turn exit lane. I turned by instinct into the left lane of the street and nearly had a head-on collision. My golden rule: when leaving a parking lot, petrol station or motorway off-ramp, do it on the right and your instinct to stay right will kick in.

➡ French law says to give way to traffic on the right, even when you're on a main road. So I advise people to ease off on the foot whenever you get to a junction.

➡ Never go below a third of a tank, even if you think there's cheaper petrol further down the road; sometimes the next station's a long way off. My approach is, don't fret about cost; you're on holiday!

If problems crop up, call the **police** (☑17).

French-registered cars have details of their insurance company printed on a little green square affixed to the windscreen.

HIRING A CAR

To hire a car in France, you'll generally need to be over 21 years old, have had a driving licence for at least a year, and have an international credit card. Drivers under 25 usually have to pay a surcharge (*frais jeune conducteur*) of €25 to €35 per day.

Car-hire companies provide mandatory third-party liability insurance, but things such as collision-damage waivers (CDW, or *assurance tous risques*) vary greatly between companies. When comparing rates and conditions, the most important thing to check is the *franchise* (deductible/excess), which for a small car is usually around €600 for damage and €800 for theft. With many companies, you can reduce the excess by half, and perhaps to zero, by paying a daily insurance supplement of up to €20. Your credit card may cover CDW if you use it to pay for the rental, but the car-hire company won't know anything about this – verify conditions and details with your credit-card issuer to be sure.

Arranging your car hire or fly/drive package before you leave home is usually considerably cheaper than a walk-in rental, but beware of website offers that don't include a CDW or you may be liable for up to 100% of the car's value.

International car-hire companies:

Avis (www.avis.com)

Budget (www.budget.fr)

EasyCar (www.easycar.com)

Europcar (www.europcar.com)

Hertz (www.hertz.com)

Sixt (www.sixt.fr)

French car-hire companies:

ADA (www.ada.fr)

DLM (www.dlm.fr)

France Cars (www.francecars.fr)

Locauto (www.locauto.fr)

Renault Rent (www.renault-rent.com)

Rent a Car (www.rentacar.fr)

Deals can be found on the internet and through companies such as the following:

Auto Europe (www.autoeurope.com)

DriveAway Holidays (www.driveaway.com.au)

Holiday Autos (www.holidayautos.co.uk)

Rental cars with automatic transmission are rare in France; book well ahead for these.

For insurance reasons, it is usually forbidden to take rental cars on ferries, eg to Corsica.

BRINGING YOUR OWN VEHICLE

A right-hand-drive vehicle brought to France from the UK or Ireland must have deflectors affixed to the headlights to avoid dazzling oncoming traffic. In the UK, information on driving in France is available from the **RAC** (www.rac.co.uk/driving-abroad/france) and the **AA** (www.theaa.com).

A foreign motor vehicle entering France must display a sticker or licence plate identifying its country of registration.

MAPS

Michelin's excellent, detailed regional driving maps are highly recommended as a companion to this book, as they will help you navigate back roads and explore alternative routes; IGN's maps are ideal for more specialised activities such as hiking and cycling. Look for both at newsagents, bookshops, airports, supermarkets, tourist offices and service stations along the autoroute.

Institut Géographique National (IGN; www.ign.fr) Publishes regional fold-out maps as well as an all-France volume, *France – Routes, Autoroutes*. Has a great variety of 1:50,000-scale hiking maps, specialised *cyclocartes* (cycling maps) and themed maps showing wine regions, museums etc.

Michelin (boutiquecartesetguides.michelin. fr) Sells excellent, tear-proof yellow-orange 1:200,000-scale regional maps tailor-made for cross-country driving, with precise coverage of smaller back roads.

ROADS & CONDITIONS

France (along with Belgium) has the densest highway network in Europe. There are four types of intercity roads:

Autoroutes (highway names beginning with A) Multilane divided highways, usually (except near Calais and Lille) with tolls (*péages*). Generously outfitted with rest stops.

Routes Nationales (N, RN) National highways. Some sections have divider strips.

Routes Départementales (D) Local highways and roads.

Road Distances (KM)

	Bayonne	Bordeaux	Brest	Caen	Cahors	Calais	Chambéry	Cherbourg	Clermont-Ferrand	Dijon	Grenoble	Lille	Lyon	Marseille	Nantes	Nice	Paris	Perpignan	Strasbourg	Toulouse
Bordeaux	184																			
Brest	811	623																		
Caen	764	568	376																	
Cahors	307	218	788	661																
Calais	164	876	710	339	875															
Chambéry	860	651	120	800	523	834														
Cherbourg	835	647	399	124	743	461	923													
Clermont-Ferrand	564	358	805	566	269	717	295	689												
Dijon	807	619	867	548	378	572	273	671	279											
Grenoble	827	657	1126	806	501	863	56	929	300	302										
Lille	997	809	725	353	808	112	767	476	650	505	798									
Lyon	831	528	1018	698	439	755	103	820	171	194	110	687								
Marseille	700	651	1271	1010	521	1067	344	1132	477	506	273	999	314							
Nantes	513	326	298	292	491	593	780	317	462	656	787	609	618	975						
Nice	858	810	1429	1168	679	1225	410	1291	636	664	337	1157	473	190	1131					
Paris	771	583	596	232	582	289	565	355	424	313	571	222	462	775	384	932				
Perpignan	499	451	1070	998	320	1149	478	1094	441	640	445	1081	448	319	773	476	857			
Strasbourg	1254	1066	1079	730	847	621	496	853	584	335	551	522	488	803	867	804	490	935		
Toulouse	300	247	866	865	116	991	565	890	890	727	533	923	536	407	568	564	699	205	1022	
Tours	536	348	490	246	413	531	611	369	369	418	618	463	449	795	197	952	238	795	721	593

Routes Communales (C, V) Minor rural roads.

The last two categories, while slower, offer some of France's most enjoyable driving experiences.

ROAD RULES

Enforcement of French traffic laws (see www.securiteroutiere.gouv.fr) has been stepped up considerably in recent years. Speed cameras are common, as are radar traps and unmarked police vehicles. Fines for many infractions are given on the spot, and serious violations can lead to the confiscation of your driving licence and car.

Speed Limits

Speed limits outside built-up areas (except where signposted otherwise):

Undivided N and D highways 80km/h (70km/h when raining)

Non-autoroute divided highways 110km/h (100km/h when raining)

Autoroutes 130km/h (110km/h when raining, 60km/h in icy conditions)

To reduce carbon emissions, autoroute speed limits have recently been reduced to 110km/h in some areas.

   Unless otherwise signposted, a limit of 50km/h applies in all areas designated as built up, no matter how rural they may appear. You must slow to 50km/h the moment you come to a white sign with a red border and a place name written on it; the speed limit applies until you pass an identical sign with a horizontal bar through it.

Alcohol

➡ Blood-alcohol limit is 0.05% (0.5g per litre of blood) – the equivalent of two glasses of wine for a 75kg adult.

➡ Police often conduct random breathalyser tests and penalties can be severe, including imprisonment.

Motorcycles

➡ Riders of any type of two-wheeled vehicle with a motor (except motor-assisted bicycles) must wear a helmet.

➡ No special licence is required to ride a motorbike whose engine is smaller than 50cc, which is why rental scooters are often rated at 49.9cc.

➡ All riders of motorcycles 125cc or larger must wear high-visibility reflective clothing measuring at least 150 sq cm on their upper bodies.

Child Seat

➡ Children under 10 are not permitted to ride in the front seat (unless the back is already occupied by other children under 10).

➡ A child under 13kg must travel in a backward-facing child seat (permitted in the front seat only for babies under 9kg and if the airbag is deactivated).

➡ Up to age 10 and/or a minimum height of 140cm, children must use a size-appropriate type of front-facing child seat or booster.

Other Rules

➡ All passengers, including those in the back seat, must wear seat belts.

Priority to the Right

Under the *priorité à droite* ('priority to the right') rule, any car entering an intersection (including a T-junction) from a road (including a tiny village backstreet) on your right has the right of way. Locals assume every driver knows this, so don't be surprised if they courteously cede the right of way when you're about to turn from an alley onto a highway – and boldly assert their rights when you're the one zipping down a main road.

   Priorité à droite is suspended (eg on arterial roads) when you pass a sign showing an upended yellow square with a black square in the middle. The same sign with a horizontal bar through the square lozenge reinstates the *priorité à droite* rule.

   When you arrive at a roundabout at which you do not have the right of way (ie the cars already in the roundabout do), you'll often see signs reading *vous n'avez pas la priorité* (you do not have right of way) or *cédez le passage* (give way).

Driving Problem-Buster

- -

I can't speak French; will that be a problem? While it's preferable to learn some French before travelling, French road signs are mostly of the 'international symbol' variety, and English is increasingly spoken among the younger generation. Our Language chapter can help you navigate some common roadside emergency situations; in a worst-case scenario, a good attitude and sign language can go a long way.

What should I do if my car breaks down? Safety first: turn on your flashers, put on a safety vest (legally required, and provided in rental-car glove compartments) and place a reflective triangle (also legally required) 30m to 100m behind your car to warn approaching motorists. Call for **emergency assistance** (☑112) or walk to the nearest orange roadside call box (placed every 2km along French autoroutes). If renting a vehicle, your car-hire company's service number may help expedite matters. If travelling in your own car, verify before leaving home whether your local auto club has reciprocal roadside-assistance arrangements in France.

What if I have an accident? For minor accidents you'll need to fill out a *Constat Amiable d'Accident Automobile* (accident statement, typically provided in rental-car glove compartments) and report the accident to your insurance and/or rental-car company. If necessary, contact the **police** (☑17).

What should I do if I get stopped by the police? Show your passport (or EU national ID card), licence and proof of insurance. See our Language chapter for some handy phrases.

What's the speed limit in France and how is it enforced? Speed limits (indicated by a black-on-white number inside a red circle) range from 30km/h in small towns to 130km/h on the fastest autoroutes. If the motorbike police pull you over, they'll fine you on the spot or direct you to the nearest gendarmerie (police station) to pay. If you're caught by a speed camera (placed at random intervals along French highways), the ticket will be sent to your rental-car agency, which will bill your credit card, or to your home address if you're driving your own vehicle. Fines depend on how much you're over the limit.

How do French tolls work? Many French autoroutes charge tolls. Take a ticket from the machine upon entering the highway and pay as you exit. Some exit booths are staffed by people; others are automated and will accept only chip-and-PIN credit cards or coins.

What if I can't find anywhere to stay? During summer and holiday periods, book accommodation in advance whenever possible. Local tourist offices can sometimes help find you a bed during normal business hours. Otherwise, try your luck at national chain hotels such as Etap and Formule 1 (p116), which are typically clustered at autoroute exits outside urban areas.

➡ Mobile phones may be used only if they are equipped with a hands-free kit or speaker-phone.

➡ Turning right on a red light is illegal.

➡ All vehicles driven in France must carry a high-visibility reflective safety vest (stored inside the vehicle, not in the trunk/boot), a reflective triangle, and a portable, single-use breathalyser kit.

➡ If you'll be driving on snowy roads, make sure you have snow chains (*chaînes neige*), required by law whenever and wherever the police post signs.

For pictures and descriptions of common French road signs, see the inside back cover of this book.

France Playlist

Bonjour Rachid Taha and Gaetan Roussel

Coeur Vagabond Gus Viseur

La Vie en Rose Édith Piaf

Minor Swing Django Reinhardt

L'Americano Akhenaton

Flower Duet from Lakmé Léo Delibes

De Bonnes Raisons Alex Beaupain

PARKING

In city centres, most on-street parking places are *payant* (metered) from about 9am to 7pm (sometimes with a break from noon to 2pm) Monday to Saturday, except bank holidays.

FUEL

Essence (petrol), also known as *carburant* (fuel), costs between €1.48 and €1.65 per litre for 95 unleaded (Sans Plomb 95 or SP95, usually available from a green pump) and €1.35 to €1.60 for diesel (*diesel, gazole* or *gasoil*, usually available from a yellow pump). Check and compare current prices countrywide at www.prix-carburants.gouv.fr.

Filling up *(faire le plein)* is most expensive at *autoroute* rest stops, and usually cheapest at hypermarkets.

Many small petrol stations close on Sunday afternoons and, even in cities, it can be hard to find a staffed station open late at night. In general, after-hours purchases (eg at hypermarkets' fully automatic, 24-hour stations) can only be made with a credit card that has an embedded PIN chip, so if all you've got is cash or a magnetic-strip credit card, you could be stuck.

SATELLITE NAVIGATION SYSTEMS

Sat-nav devices can be helpful in navigating your way around France. They're commonly available at car-rental agencies, or you can bring your own from home. Accuracy is more dependable on main highways than in small villages or on back roads; in rural areas, don't hesitate to fall back on common sense, road signs and a good Michelin map if your sat nav seems to be leading you astray.

SAFETY

Never leave anything valuable inside your car, even in the boot trunk. Note that thieves can easily identify rental cars, as they have a distinctive number on the licence plate.

Theft is especially prevalent in the south. In cities such as Marseille and Nice, occasional aggressive theft from cars stopped at red lights is also an issue.

RADIO

For news, tune in to the French-language France Info (105.5MHz; www.franceinfo.fr) and multilanguage RFI (738kHz or 89MHz in Paris; www.rfi.fr). Popular national FM music stations include **NRJ** (www.nrj.fr), **Virgin** (www.virginradio.fr), **La Radio Plus** (www.laradioplus.com) and **Nostalgie** (www.nostalgie.fr).

In many areas, Autoroute Info (107.7MHz; www.autorouteinfo.fr) has round-the-clock traffic information.

France Travel Guide

GETTING THERE & AWAY

AIR

International Airports

Rental cars are available at all international airports listed here.

Paris Charles de Gaulle (CDG; www.aeroportsdeparis.fr)

Paris Orly (ORY; www.aeroportsdeparis.fr)

Aéroport de Bordeaux (www.bordeaux.aeroport.fr)

Aéroport de Lille (www.lille.aeroport.fr)

Aéroport Lyon-Saint Exupéry (www.lyonaeroports.com)

EuroAirport (Basel-Mulhouse-Freiburg; www.euroairport.com)

Aéroport Nantes Atlantique (www.nantes.aeroport.fr)

Aéroport Nice Côte d'Azur (https://societe.nice.aeroport.fr)

Aéroport International Strasbourg (www.strasbourg.aeroport.fr)

Aéroport Toulouse-Blagnac (www.toulouse.aeroport.fr)

CAR & MOTORCYCLE

Entering France from other parts of the EU is usually a breeze – no border checkpoints and no customs – thanks to the Schengen Agreement, signed by all of France's neighbours except the UK, the Channel Islands and Andorra. For these three, old-fashioned document and customs checks are still the norm when exiting France (as well as when entering from Andorra).

Channel Tunnel

The Channel Tunnel (Chunnel), inaugurated in 1994, is the first dry-land link between England and France since the last ice age.

High-speed **Eurotunnel Le Shuttle** (☎France 08 10 63 03 04, UK 08443 35 35 35; www.eurotunnel.com) trains whisk bicycles, motorcycles, cars and coaches in 35 minutes from Folkestone through the Channel Tunnel to Coquelles, 5km southwest of Calais. Shuttles run 24 hours a day, with up to three departures an hour during peak periods. LPG and CNG tanks are not permitted, meaning gas-powered cars and many campers and caravans have to travel by ferry.

Eurotunnel sets its fares the way budget airlines do: the further in advance you book and the lower the demand for a particular crossing, the less you pay; same-day fares can cost a small fortune. Fares for a car, including up to nine passengers, start at £30 (€37).

SEA

Some ferry companies have started setting fares the way budget airlines do: the longer in advance you book and the lower the demand for a particular sailing, the less you pay. Seasonal demand is a crucial factor (Christmas, Easter, UK and French school holidays, and July and August are especially busy), as is the time of day (an early-evening ferry can cost much more than one at 4am). People under 25 and over 60 may qualify for discounts.

To get the best fares, check **Ferry Savers** (www.ferrysavers.com).

Foot passengers are not allowed on Dover–Boulogne, Dover–Dunkirk or Dover–Calais car ferries except for daytime (and, from Calais to Dover, evening) crossings run by P&O Ferries. On ferries that do allow foot passengers, taking a bicycle is usually free.

Several ferry companies ply the waters between Corsica and Italy.

TRAIN

Rail services link France with virtually every country in Europe. The **Eurostar** (www.eurostar.com) whisks passengers from London to Paris in 2¼ hours.

You can book tickets and get train information from **Rail Europe** (www.raileurope.com). In France ticketing is handled by the national railway company **SNCF** (www.sncf.com). High-speed train travel between France and the UK, Belgium, the Netherlands, Germany and Austria is covered by **Railteam** (www.railteam.co.uk) and **TGV-Europe** (www.tgv-europe.com).

Avis (www.avis.fr), in partnership with **SNCF** (www.voyages-sncf.com/train/train-avis), has rental-car agencies in most major French railway stations. Cars booked through the SNCF website may be picked up from an SNCF representative after hours if the Avis office is closed.

DIRECTORY A–Z

ACCOMMODATION

Be it a fairy-tale château, a boutique hideaway or floating pod on a lake, France has accommodation to suit every taste and pocket.

Categories

As a rule of thumb, budget covers everything from basic hostels to small family-run places; midrange means a few extra creature comforts such as a lift; while top-end places stretch from luxury five-star palaces with air-conditioning, swimming pools and restaurants to boutique-chic Alpine chalets.

Costs

Accommodation costs vary wildly between seasons and regions: what will buy you a night in a romantic *chambre d'hôte* (B&B) in the countryside may get a dorm bed in a major city or high-profile ski resort.

Reservations

Midrange, top-end and many budget hotels require a credit card number to secure an advance reservation made by phone; some hostels do not take bookings. Many tourist offices can advise on availability and reserve for you, often for a fee of €5 and usually only if you stop by in person.

Seasons

➡ In ski resorts, high season is Christmas, New Year and the February–March school holidays.

➡ On the coast, high season is summer, particularly August.

➡ Hotels in inland cities often charge low-season rates in summer.

➡ Rates often drop outside the high season – in some cases by as much as 50%.

➡ In business-oriented hotels in cities, rooms are most expensive from Monday to Thursday and cheaper over the weekend.

➡ In the Alps, hotels usually close between seasons, from around May to mid-June and from mid-September to early December; many addresses in Corsica only open Easter to October.

B&Bs

For charm, a heartfelt *bienvenue* (welcome) and solid home cooking, it's hard to beat France's privately run *chambres d'hôte* (B&Bs) – urban rarities but as common as muck in rural areas. By law a *chambre d'hôte* must have no more than five rooms and breakfast must be included in the price; some hosts prepare a meal (*table d'hôte*) for an extra charge of around €30 including wine. Pick up lists

Practicalities

Time France uses the 24-hour clock and is on Central European Time, which is one hour ahead of GMT/UTC. During daylight-saving time, which runs from the last Sunday in March to the last Sunday in October, France is two hours ahead of GMT/UTC.

TV & DVD TV is Secam; DVDs are zone 2; videos work on the PAL system.

Weights and measures France uses the metric system.

Sleeping Price Ranges

The following price ranges refer to a double room with private bathroom in high season (breakfast is not included, except at B&Bs).

€	less than €90
€€	€90–190
€€€	more than €190

of *chambres d' hôte* at tourist offices, or consult the following websites:

Bienvenue à la Ferme (www.bienvenue -a-la-ferme.com) Farmstays.

Chambres d'hôtes de Charme (www. guidesdecharme.com) Boutique B&Bs.

Chambres d'Hôtes France (www.chambresdhotesfrance.com)

en France (www.bbfrance.com) B&Bs and *gîtes* (self-catering cottages).

Fleurs de Soleil (www.fleursdesoleil.fr) Stylish *maisons d'hôte*, mainly in rural France.

Gîtes de France (www.gites-de-france.com) France's primary umbrella organisation for B&Bs and *gîtes*. Search for properties by region, theme (with kids, by the sea, gourmet, etc) or activity (fishing, wine tasting etc) or facilities (pool, dishwasher, fireplace, baby equipment etc).

Guides de Charme (www.guidesdecharme. com) Upmarket B&Bs.

Samedi Midi Éditions (www.samedimidi. com) Chambres d'hôte organised by location or theme.

Camping

Be it a Mongolian yurt, boutique tree house or simple canvas beneath stars, camping in France is in vogue. Thousands of well-equipped campgrounds dot the country, many considerately placed by rivers, lakes and the sea.

➡ Most campgrounds open March or April to late September or October; popular spots fill up fast in summer so it is wise to call ahead.

➡ 'Sites' refer to fixed-price deals for two people including a tent and a car. Otherwise the price is broken down per adult/tent/car. Factor in a few extra euro per night for *taxe de séjour* (holiday tax) and electricity.

➡ Euro-economisers should look out for local, good-value but no-frills *campings municipaux* (municipal campgrounds).

➡ Many campgrounds rent out mobile homes with mod cons such as heating, kitchen and TV.

➡ Pitching up 'wild' in nondesignated spots *(camping sauvage)* is illegal in France.

➡ Campground offices often close during the day.

➡ Accessing many campgrounds without your own transport can be slow and costly, or simply impossible.

Websites with campsite listings searchable by location, theme and facilities:

Camping en France (www.camping.fr)

Camping France (www.campingfrance.com)

Guide du Camping (www.guideducamp ing.com)

HPA Guide (http://camping.hpaguide.com)

Hostels

Hostels in France range from funky to threadbare, although with a wave of design-driven, up-to-the-minute hostels opening in Paris, Marseille and other big cities, hip hang-outs with perks aplenty seem to easily outweigh the threadbare these days.

➡ In university towns, *foyers d'étudiant* (student dormitories) are sometimes converted for use by travellers during summer.

➡ A dorm bed in an *auberge de jeunesse* (hostel) costs €20 to €50 in Paris, and anything from €15 to €40 in the provinces, depending on location, amenities and facilities; sheets are always included, as is breakfast more often than not.

➡ To prevent outbreaks of bedbugs, sleeping bags are not permitted.

➡ Hostels by the sea or in the mountains sometimes offer seasonal outdoor activities.

➡ French hostels are 100% nonsmoking.

Book Your Stay Online

For more accommodation reviews by Lonely Planet authors, check out http://hotels.lonelyplanet.com. You'll find independent reviews, as well as recommendations on the best places to stay. Best of all, you can book online.

Hotels

We have tried to feature well-situated, independent hotels that offer good value, a warm welcome, at least a bit of charm and a palpable sense of place.

➡ Hotels in France are rated with one to five stars, although the ratings are based on highly objective criteria (eg the size of the entry hall), not the quality of the service, the decor or cleanliness.

➡ French hotels almost never include breakfast in their rates. Unless specified otherwise, prices quoted don't include breakfast, which costs around €8/12/25 in a budget/midrange/top-end hotel.

➡ When you book, hotels usually ask for a credit card number; some require a deposit.

➡ A double room generally has one double bed; a room with twin beds (deux lits) is usually more expensive, as is a room with a bathtub instead of a shower.

➡ Feather pillows are practically nonexistent in France, even in top-end hotels.

➡ All hotel restaurant terraces allow smoking; if you are sensitive to smoke, you may need to sit inside.

Chain Hotels

Chain hotels stretch from nondescript establishments near the autoroute (motorway, highway) to central four-star hotels with character. Most conform to certain standards of decor, service and facilities (air-conditioning, free wi-fi, 24-hour check-in etc), and offer competitive rates as well as last-minute, weekend and/or online deals. Countrywide biggies:

B&B Hôtels (www.hotel-bb.com) Cheap motel-style digs.

Best Western (www.bestwestern.com) Independent two- to four-star hotels, each with its own local character.

Campanile (www.campanile.com) Good value hotels geared up for families.

Citôtel (www.citotel.com) Independent two and three-star hotels.

Contact Hôtel (www.contact-hotel.com) Inexpensive two- and three-star hotels.

Etap (www.etaphotel.com) Ubiquitous chain.

Formule 1 (www.hotelformule1.com) Nondescript roadside cheapie.

Ibis (www.ibishotel.com) Midrange pick.

Inter-Hotel (www.inter-hotel.fr) Two- and three-star hotels, some quite charming.

Kyriad (www.kyriad.com) Comfortable midrange choices.

Novotel (www.novotel.com) Family-friendly.

Première Classe (www.premiereclasse.com) Motel-style accommodation.

Sofitel (www.sofitel.com) Range of top-end hotels in major French cities.

ELECTRICITY

European two-pin plugs are standard. France has 230V at 50Hz AC (you may need a transformer for 110V electrical appliances).

Type E
220V/50Hz

FOOD

Food-happy France has a seemingly endless variety of eateries; categories listed here are found throughout the country: The Eating & Sleeping sections of this guide include phone numbers for places that require reservations (typically higher end bistros or family-run enterprises such as tables d'hôte).

Auberge Country inn serving traditional fare, often attached to a B&B or small hotel.

Ferme auberge Working farm that cooks up meals – only dinner usually – from local farm products.

Eating Price Ranges

Price indicators refer to the average cost of a two-course meal, be it an *entrée* (starter) and *plat* (main course) or main and dessert, or a two- or three-course *menu* (set meal at a fixed price).

€	less than €20
€€	€20–40
€€€	more than €40

Bistro (also spelt *bistrot*) Anything from a pub or bar with snacks and light meals to a small, fully fledged restaurant.

Brasserie Much like a cafe except it serves full meals, drinks and coffee from morning until 11pm or later. Typical fare includes *choucroute* (sauerkraut) and *moules frites* (mussels and fries).

Restaurant Born in Paris in the 18th century, restaurants today serve lunch and dinner five or six days a week.

Cafe Basic light snacks as well as drinks.

Crêperie (also *galetterie*) Casual address specialising in sweet crêpes and savoury *galettes* (buckwheat crêpes).

Salon de Thé Trendy tearoom often serving light lunches (quiche, salads, cakes, tarts, pies and pastries) as well as black and herbal teas.

Table d'hôte (literally 'host's table') Some of the most charming B&Bs serve *table d'hôte* too, a delicious homemade meal of set courses with little or no choice.

INTERNET ACCESS

➡ Wi-fi (pronounced 'wee-fee' in French) is available at major airports, in most hotels, and at many cafes, restaurants, museums and tourist offices.

➡ In cities free wi-fi is available in hundreds of public places, including parks, libraries and municipal buildings. In Paris look for a purple 'Zone Wi-Fi' sign. To connect, select the 'PARIS_WI-FI_' network. Sessions are limited to two hours (renewable). For complete details and a map of hotspots, see www.paris.fr/wifi.

➡ To search for free wi-fi hotspots in France, visit www.hotspot-locations.com.

➡ Tourist offices is some larger cities, including Lyon and Bordeaux, rent out pocket-sized mobile wi-fi devices that you carry around with you, ensuring a fast wi-fi connection while roaming the city.

➡ Alternatively, rent a mobile wi-fi device online before leaving home and arrange for it to be delivered by post to your hotel in France through HipPocketWifi (http://hippocketwifi.com), Travel WiFi (http://travel-wifi.com) or My Webspot (http://my-webspot.com).

➡ Co-working cafes providing unlimited, fast internet access are increasingly rife; at least one can usually be tracked down in cities. Expect to pay about €5 per hour for a desk, plug and unlimited hot drinks and snacks.

LGBT+ TRAVELLERS

The rainbow flag flies high in France, a country that left its closet long before many of its European neighbours. *Laissez-faire* perfectly sums up France's liberal attitude towards homosexuality and people's private lives in general; in part because of a long tradition of public tolerance towards unconventional lifestyles. Bordeaux, Lille, Lyon, Montpellier, Toulouse and many other towns have an active queer scene. Attitudes towards homosexuality tend to be more conservative in the countryside and villages.

Publications

Damron (www.damron.com) Has published English-language travel guides since the 1960s, including *Damron Women's Traveller* for lesbians and *Damron Men's Travel Guide* for gays.

Spartacus International Gay Guide (www.spartacusworld.com) A male-only guide to just about every country in the world, with more than 70 pages devoted to France, almost half of which cover Paris. There's a smartphone app too.

Websites

Gaipied (www.gayvox.com/guide3) Online travel guide to France, with listings by region, by Gayvox.

Gay Travel & Life in France (www.gay-france.net) Insider tips on gay life in France.

Tipping Guide

By law, restaurant and bar prices are *service compris* (include a 15% service charge), so there is no need to leave a *pourboire* (tip). If you were extremely satisfied with the service, however, you can – as many locals do – leave a small 'extra' tip for your waiter or waitress.

Hotels €1 to €2 per bag is standard; gratuity for cleaning staff is at your discretion.

Bars No tips for drinks at bar; round to nearest euro for drinks served at table.

Restaurants For decent service 10%.

Pubic toilets For super-clean, sparkling toilets with music, €0.50 at most.

Tours For excellent guides, €1 to €2 per person.

Tasse de Thé (www.tassedethe.com) A *webzine lesbien* with lots of useful links.

MONEY

ATMs

Automated Teller Machines (ATMs) – known as *distributeurs automatiques de billets* (DAB) or *points d'argent* in French – are the cheapest and most convenient way to get money. ATMs connected to international networks are situated in all cities and towns and usually offer an excellent exchange rate.

Cash

You always get a better exchange rate in-country, but it is a good idea to arrive in France with enough euros to take a taxi to a hotel if you have to.

Credit & Debits Cards

➡ Credit and debit cards, accepted almost everywhere in France, are convenient, relatively secure and usually offer a better exchange rate than travellers cheques or cash exchanges.

➡ Credit cards issued in France have embedded chips – you have to type in a PIN to make a purchase.

➡ Visa, MasterCard and Amex can be used in shops and supermarkets and for train travel, car hire and motorway tolls.

➡ Don't assume that you can pay for a meal or a budget hotel with a credit card – enquire first.

➡ Cash advances are a supremely convenient way to stay stocked up with euros, but getting cash with a credit card involves both fees

(sometimes US$10 or more) and interest – ask your credit-card issuer for details. Debit-card fees are usually much lower.

Moneychangers

➡ Commercial banks charge up to €5 per foreign-currency transaction – if they even bother to offer exchange services any more.

➡ In major cities, *bureaux de change* (exchange bureaus) are faster and easier, open longer hours and often give better rates than banks.

OPENING HOURS

Opening hours vary throughout the year. We list high-season opening hours, but remember these longer summer hours often decrease in shoulder and low seasons.

Banks 9am–noon and 2pm–5pm Monday to Friday or Tuesday to Saturday

Bars 7pm–1am

Cafes 7am–11pm

Clubs 10pm–3am, 4am or 5am Thursday to Saturday

Restaurants Noon–2.30pm and 7pm–11pm six days a week

Shops 10am–noon and 2pm–7pm Monday to Saturday; longer, and including Sunday, for shops in ZTIs (international tourist zones)

PUBLIC HOLIDAYS

The following *jours fériés* (public holidays) are observed in France:

New Year's Day (Jour de l'An) 1 January

Easter Sunday & Monday (Pâques & Lundi de Pâques) Late March/April

May Day (Fête du Travail) 1 May

Victoire 1945 8 May

Ascension Thursday (Ascension) May; on the 40th day after Easter

Pentecost/Whit Sunday & Whit Monday (Pentecôte & Lundi de Pentecôte) Mid-May to mid-June; on the seventh Sunday after Easter

Bastille Day/National Day (Fête Nationale) 14 July

Assumption Day (Assomption) 15 August

All Saints' Day (Toussaint) 1 November

Remembrance Day (L'onze Novembre) 11 November

Christmas (Noël) 25 December

SAFE TRAVEL

France is generally a safe place to travel, though crime has risen substantially in recent years. Property crime is much more common than physical violence; it's extremely unlikely that you will be assaulted while walking down the street.

Hunting is traditional and commonplace throughout rural France, and the season runs from September to February. If you see signs reading 'chasseurs' or 'chasse gardée' strung up or tacked into trees, think twice about wandering into the area.

Natural Dangers

➡ There are powerful tides and strong undertows at many places along the Atlantic coast, from the Spanish border north to Brittany and Normandy.

➡ Only swim in *zones de baignade surveillée* (beaches monitored by life guards).

➡ Be aware of tide times and the high-tide mark if walking on a beach.

➡ Check the weather report before setting out on a long walk and be prepared for sudden temperature drops if you're heading into the high country of the Alps or Pyrenees.

➡ Avalanches pose a danger in the Alps.

Theft

There's no need to travel in fear, but it is worth taking a few simple precautions against theft.

➡ Break-ins to parked cars are not uncommon. Never leave anything valuable inside your car, even in the boot (trunk).

➡ Aggressive theft from cars stopped at red lights is occasionally a problem, especially in Marseille and Nice. As a precaution, lock your car doors and roll up the windows in major urban areas.

➡ Pickpocketing and bag snatching are prevalent in big cities, particularly Paris. Be especially vigilant for bag-snatchers at outdoor cafes and beaches.

TELEPHONE

Mobile Phones

➡ French mobile phone numbers begin with ☎06 or ☎07.

➡ France uses GSM 900/1800, which is compatible with the rest of Europe and Australia but not with the North American GSM 1900 or the totally different system in Japan (though some North Americans have tri-band phones that work here).

➡ Check with your service provider about roaming charges – dialling a mobile phone from a fixed-line phone or another mobile can be incredibly expensive.

➡ It is usually cheaper to buy a local SIM card from a French provider such as Orange, SFR, Bouygues or Free Mobile, which gives you a local phone number. To do this, ensure your phone is unlocked.

➡ If you already have a compatible phone, you can slip in a SIM card and rev it up with prepaid credit, though this is likely to run out fast as domestic prepaid calls cost about €0.50 per minute.

➡ Recharge cards are sold at most *tabacs* (tobacconist-newsagents), supermarkets and online through websites such as Topengo (www.topengo.fr) or Sim-OK (https://recharge.sim-ok.com).

Phone Codes

Calling France from abroad Dial your country's international access code, then 33 (France's country code), then the 10-digit local number *without* the initial zero.

Calling internationally from France Dial ☎00 (the international access code), the *indicatif* (country code), the area code (without the initial zero if there is one) and the local number. Some country codes are posted in public telephones.

Directory enquiries For national *service des renseignements* (directory inquiries) dial ☑11 87 12 or use the service for free online at www.118712.fr.

International directory inquiries For numbers outside France, dial ☑11 87 00.

Phone Cards

➡ Public phones still exist, but are hard to find. Phones accept calling cards or credit cards.

➡ Emergency numbers can be dialled from public phones without a card.

➡ Prepaid calling cards with codes *(tickets téléphones)*, sold at *tabacs* (tobacconists), are the cheapest way to call. When purchasing, *tabacs* can tell you which type is best for the country you want to call.

➡ Using calling cards from a home phone is much cheaper than using them from public phones or mobile phones.

➡ Hotels, *gîtes*, hostels and *chambres d'hôte* are free to meter their calls as they like. The surcharge is usually around €0.30 per minute but can be higher.

TOILETS

Public toilets around France are signposted WC or toilettes. These range from spiffy 24-hour mechanical self-cleaning toilets costing around €0.50 to hole-in-the-floor *toilettes à la turque* (squat toilets) at older establishments and motorway stops. In the most basic places you may need to supply your own paper.

The French are more blasé about unisex toilets than elsewhere, so save your blushes when tiptoeing past

TOURIST INFORMATION

Almost every city, town and village has an *office de tourisme* (a tourist office run by some unit of local government) or *syndicat d'initiative* (a tourist office run by an organisation of local merchants). Both are excellent resources and can supply you with local maps as well as details on accommodation, restaurants and activities.

Useful websites include the following:

French Government Tourist Office (www.france.fr/en) The low-down on sights,

activities, transport and special-interest holidays in all of France's regions.

French Tourist Offices (www.tourisme. fr) Website of tourist offices in France, with mountains of inspirational information organised by theme and region.

TRAVELLERS WITH DISABILITIES

While France presents evident challenges for *visiteurs handicapés* (disabled visitors), particularly those with mobility issues – cobblestones, cafe-lined streets that are a nightmare to navigate in a wheelchair *(fauteuil roulant)*, a lack of kerb ramps, older public facilities and many budget hotels without lifts – don't let that stop you from visiting. Efforts are being made to improve the situation and with a little careful planning, a hassle-free accessible stay is possible.

Whether you are looking for wheelchair-friendly accommodation, sights, attractions or restaurants, these associations and agencies can help:

Accès Plus (☑03 69 32 26 26, 08 90 64 06 50; www.accessibilite.sncf.com) The SNCF assistance service for rail travellers with disabilities. Can advise on station accessibility and arrange a *fauteuil roulant* or help getting on or off a train.

Tourisme et Handicaps (☑01 44 11 10 41; www.tourisme-handicaps.org; 43 rue Marx Dormoy, 18e) Issues the 'Tourisme et Handicap' label to tourist sites, restaurants and hotels that comply with strict accessibility and usability standards. Different symbols indicate the sort of access afforded to people with physical, mental, hearing and/or visual disabilities.

VISAS

For up-to-date details on visa requirements, see the website of the Ministère des Affaires Étrangères (Ministry of Foreign Affairs; www.diplomatie.gouv.fr/en) and click 'Coming to France'. Visas are not required for EU nationals or citizens of Iceland, Norway and Switzerland, and are required only for stays greater than 90 days for citizens of Australia, the USA, Canada, Hong Kong, Israel, Japan, Malaysia, New Zealand, Singapore, South Korea and many Latin American countries.

Language

The sounds used in spoken French can almost all be found in English. There are a couple of exceptions: nasal vowels (represented in our pronunciation guides by o or u followed by an almost inaudible nasal consonant sound m, n or ng), the 'funny' *u* (ew in our guides) and the deep-in-the-throat *r*. Bearing these few points in mind and reading our pronunciation guides below as if they were English, you'll be understood just fine.

BASICS

Hello.	*Bonjour.*	bon·zhoor
Goodbye.	*Au revoir.*	o·rer·vwa
Yes./No.	*Oui./Non.*	wee/non
Excuse me.	*Excusez-moi.*	ek·skew·zay·mwa
Sorry.	*Pardon.*	par·don
Please.	*S'il vous plaît.*	seel voo play
Thank you.	*Merci.*	mair·see

You're welcome.
De rien.　　　　　　der ree·en

Do you speak English?
Parlez-vous anglais?　par·lay·voo ong·glay

I don't understand.
Je ne comprends pas.　zher ner kom·pron pa

How much is this?
C'est combien?　　　say kom·byun

ACCOMMODATION

Do you have any rooms available?
Est-ce que vous avez　es·ker voo za·vay
des chambres libres?　day shom·brer lee·brer

How much is it per night/person?
Quel est le prix　　　kel ay ler pree
par nuit/personne?　par nwee/per·son

DIRECTIONS

Can you show me (on the map)?
Pouvez-vous m'indiquer　poo·vay·voo mun·dee·kay
(sur la carte)?　　　(sewr la kart)

Where's ...?
Où est ...?　　　　oo ay ...

EATING & DRINKING

What would you recommend?
Qu'est-ce que vous　kes·ker voo
conseillez?　　　kon·say·yay

I'd like ..., please.
Je voudrais ...,　　zher voo·dray ...
s'il vous plaît.　　seel voo play

I'm a vegetarian.
Je suis végétarien/　zher swee vay·zhay·ta·ryun/
végétarienne.　　vay·zhay·ta·ryen (m/f)

Please bring the bill.
Apportez-moi　　a·por·tay·mwa
l'addition,　　la·dee·syon
s'il vous plaît.　　seel voo play

EMERGENCIES

Help!
Au secours!　　　o skoor

I'm lost.
Je suis perdu/perdue.　zhe swee·pair·dew (m/f)

I'm ill.
Je suis malade.　　zher swee ma·lad

Want More?

For in-depth language information and handy phrases, check out Lonely Planet's *French Phrasebook*. You'll find it at **shop.lonelyplanet.com**, or you can buy Lonely Planet's iPhone phrasebooks at the Apple App Store.

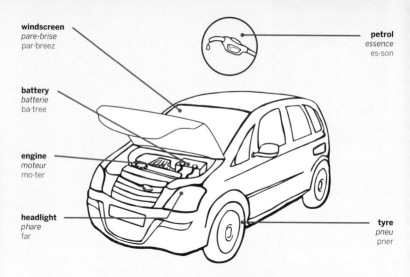

windscreen
pare-brise
par·breez

petrol
essence
es·son

battery
batterie
ba·tree

engine
moteur
mo·ter

headlight
phare
far

tyre
pneu
pner

Signs

Cédez la Priorité	Give Way
Sens Interdit	No Entry
Entrée	Entrance
Péage	Toll
Sens Unique	One Way
Sortie	Exit

Call the police!
Appelez la police!   a·play la po·lees

Call a doctor!
Appelez un médecin!   a·play un mayd·sun

ON THE ROAD

I'd like to hire a/an ...	*Je voudrais louer ...*	zher voo·dray loo·way ...
4WD	*un quatre-quatre*	un kat·kat
automatic/ manual	*une auto- matique/ manuel*	ewn o·to· ma·teek/ ma·nwel
motorbike	*une moto*	ewn mo·to

How much is it daily/weekly?
Quel est le tarif par jour/semaine?   kel ay ler ta·reef par zhoor/ser·men

Does that include insurance?
Est-ce que l'assurance est comprise?   es·ker la·sew·rons ay kom·preez

Does that include mileage?
Est-ce que le kilométrage est compris?   es·ker ler kee·lo·may·trazh ay kom·pree

What's the speed limit?
Quelle est la vitesse maximale permise?   kel ay la vee·tes mak·see·mal per·meez

Is this the road to ...?
C'est la route pour ...?   say la root poor ...

Can I park here?
Est-ce que je peux stationner ici?   es·ker zher per sta·syo·nay ee·see

Where's a service station?
Où est-ce qu'il y a une station-service?   oo es·keel ya ewn sta·syon·ser·vees

Please fill it up.
Le plein, s'il vous plaît.   ler plun seel voo play

I'd like (20) litres.
Je voudrais (vingt) litres.   zher voo·dray (vung) lee·trer

Please check the oil/water.
Contrôlez l'huile/l'eau, s'il vous plaît.   kon·tro·lay lweel/lo seel voo play

I need a mechanic.
J'ai besoin d'un mécanicien.   zhay ber·zwun dun may·ka·nee·syun

The car/motorbike has broken down.
La voiture/moto est tombée en panne.   la vwa·tewr/mo·to ay tom·bay on pan

I had an accident.
J'ai eu un accident.   zhay ew un ak·see·don

BEHIND THE SCENES

SEND US YOUR FEEDBACK

We love to hear from travellers – your comments help make our books better. We read every word, and we guarantee that your feedback goes straight to the authors. Visit **lonelyplanet. com/contact** to submit your updates and suggestions.

Note: We may edit, reproduce and incorporate your comments in Lonely Planet products such as guidebooks, websites and digital products, so let us know if you don't want your comments reproduced or your name acknowledged. For a copy of our privacy policy visit lonelyplanet.com/privacy.

ACKNOWLEDGMENTS

Climate map data adapted from Peel MC, Finlayson BL & McMahon TA (2007) 'Updated World Map of the Köppen-Geiger Climate Classification', Hydrology and Earth System Sciences, 11, 163344.

Cover photographs: (front) Lavender fields, Provence, Marcutti/Getty Images ©; (back) Menton, French Riviera, RudyBalasko/Getty Images ©

THIS BOOK

This 2nd edition of Lonely Planet's *Provence & Southeast France Road Trips* guidebook was researched and written by Oliver Berry, Jean-Bernard Carillet, Gregor Clark, Hugh McNaughtan and Nicola Williams. The previous edition was written by Oliver Berry, Gregor Clark, Emilie Filou, Donna Wheeler and Nicola Williams. This guidebook was produced by the following:

Destination Editor Daniel Fahey

Senior Product Editor Genna Patterson

Regional Senior Cartographer Mark Griffiths

Product Editors Alison Ridgway, Ross Taylor

Book Designer Mazzy Prinsep

Assisting Editor Melanie Dankel

Assisting Cartographer Rachel Imeson

Cover Researcher Naomi Parker

Thanks to Kate Chapman, Anne Mason, Jenna Myers, Charles Wong

OUR STORY

A beat-up old car, a few dollars in the pocket and a sense of adventure. In 1972 that's all Tony and Maureen Wheeler needed for the trip of a lifetime – across Europe and Asia overland to Australia. It took several months, and at the end – broke but inspired – they sat at their kitchen table writing and stapling together their first travel guide, *Across Asia on the Cheap*. Within a week they'd sold 1500 copies. Lonely Planet was born.

Today, Lonely Planet has offices in Melbourne, London and Oakland, with more than 600 staff and writers. We share Tony's belief that 'a great guidebook should do three things: inform, educate and amuse'.

INDEX

000 Map pages

000 Map pages

NICOLA WILLIAMS

Border-hopping is way of life for British writer, runner, foodie, art aficionado and mum-of-three, Nicola, who has lived in a French village on the southern side of Lake Geneva for more than a decade. Nicola has authored more than 50 guidebooks for Lonely Planet, and covers France as a destination expert for the *Telegraph*. She also writes for the *Independent*, *Guardian*, Lonely Planet's *Traveller* magazine, *French Magazine*, *Cool Camping France* and others. Catch her on the road on Twitter and Instagram @tripalong.

OUR WRITERS

OLIVER BERRY

Oliver is a writer and photographer from Cornwall. He has worked for Lonely Planet for more than a decade, covering destinations from Cornwall to the Cook Islands, and has worked on more than 30 guidebooks. He is also a regular contributor to many newspapers and magazines, including Lonely Planet *Traveller*. His writing has won several awards, including the *Guardian* Young Travel Writer of the Year and the *TNT Magazine* People's Choice Award.

GREGOR CLARK

Gregor is a US-based writer whose love of foreign languages and curiosity about what's around the next bend have taken him to dozens of countries on five continents. Chronic wanderlust has also led him to visit all 50 states and most Canadian provinces on countless road trips through his native North America. Since 2000, Gregor has regularly contributed to Lonely Planet guides, with a focus on Europe and the Americas.

JEAN-BERNARD CARILLET

Jean-Bernard is a Paris-based freelance writer and photographer who specialises in Africa, France, Turkey, the Indian Ocean, the Caribbean and the Pacific. He loves adventure, remote places, islands, outdoors, archaeological sites and food. His insatiable wanderlust has taken him to 114 countries across six continents, and it shows no sign of waning. It has inspired lots of articles and photos for travel magazines and some 70 Lonely Planet guidebooks, both in English and in French.

HUGH MCNAUGHTAN

A former English lecturer, Hugh swapped grant applications for visa applications, and turned his love of travel into a full-time thing. Having done a bit of restaurant-reviewing in his home town (Melbourne) he's now eaten his way across four continents. He's never happier than when on the road with his two daughters. Except perhaps on the cricket field.

 MORE WRITERS

Published by Lonely Planet Publications Pty Ltd
ABN 36 005 607 983
2nd edition – June 2019
ISBN 978 1 78657 395 7
© Lonely Planet 2019   Photographs © as indicated 2019
10 9 8 7 6 5 4 3 2 1
Printed in China

Although the authors and Lonely Planet have taken all reasonable care in preparing this book, we make no warranty about the accuracy or completeness of its content and, to the maximum extent permitted, disclaim all liability arising from its use.